Setting Up Your Own Woodworking Shop

Bill Stankus

 Sterling Publishing Co., Inc. New York

Dedication

This book is dedicated to Katherine

Grateful acknowledgment is made to Robert Scharff for his kind permission to reprint material found on pages 197–222 from *Workshop Formulas, Tips & Data* by Kenneth M. Swezey, updated by Robert Scharff, © 1979 by Robert Scharff.

Library of Congress Cataloging-in-Publication Data

Stankus, Bill.
    Setting up your own woodworking shop / by Bill Stankus.
       p.   cm.
    Includes index.
    ISBN 0-8069-8314-0
    1. Woodwork—Amateurs' manuals. 2. Workshops—Equipment and supplies—Amateurs' manuals. 3. Woodworking tools—Amateurs' manuals. I. Title.
  TT185.S69 1993
  684'.08'028—dc20
                                    92-43351
                                    CIP

10 9 8 7 6 5 4 3 2 1

Published by Sterling Publishing Company, Inc.
387 Park Avenue South, New York, N.Y. 10016
© 1993 by Bill Stankus
Distributed in Canada by Sterling Publishing
℅ Canadian Manda Group, P.O. Box 920, Station U
Toronto, Ontario, Canada M8Z 5P9
Distributed in Great Britain and Europe by Cassell PLC
Villiers House, 41/47 Strand, London WC2N 5JE, England
Distributed in Australia by Capricorn Link Ltd
P.O. Box 665, Lane Cove, NSW 2066
Manufactured in the United States of America
All rights reserved

Sterling ISBN 0-8069-8314-0

Contents

Acknowledgments

There are certain people that I would like to thank for their assistance, ideas, observations and for allowing me to visit and take photographs in their workshops: Jon Arno, Bob Baker, Bill Daley, John Danielson, Dick Dermody, Scott Gruenberg, Jim Kirchner, Nick Kovacs, Pete Kolettis, Mark Nathenson, Monty Parker, Norm Petersen, Dean Slindee, and George Stefureac.

I would especially like to thank Katherine Stankus for her support, encouragement, and editorial assistance. Without her help, this book couldn't have been published.

Commercial photographs and technical information were generously furnished by the following people and companies:

Keith Scoggins at Ryobi Motor Products Corp.
David Hazelwood at Emerson
Chuck Olsen at Olsen Saw Blade Co.
John Pickhardt at Flordia Pneumatic
Mike Brainerd at Dremel
Christopher Taylor at Taylor Design Group
Ken Grisley at Leigh Industries
John McConegly at J.D.S. Co.
Steven Holley at Delta Corp.
David Draves at Woodcraft Supply Co.
Ron Clark at Leeson Electric Corp.
Debbie Williams at Ferris Machinery
Ken Marg at Accuspray Inc.
Mary Beth Buckman at Wagner Spray Tech Corp.
Brad Witt at Woodhaven Tools
Paul Starret at AMI
Ray St. Louis at R. F. St. Louis Associates, Inc.
Robin Gavoor at Shopcarts
Frank Schepens at Lee Valley Tools Ltd.
Roger Thompson at Biesemeyer Manufacturing Corp.
Darryl Keil at Vacuum Pressing Systems, Inc.
Sanford Zimmerman at Edge Finisher Corp.
John Fennell at Badger Air Brush
Bill Taylor at Black & Decker
Cynthia Sawyers at Porter-Cable
Richard Biedinger at Senco Fastening Systems
Vic Wisniewski at Tyee Forest Products Co.
Joy Daum at Shopsmith
Torbin Helshoj at Laguna Tools
Tim Hewitt at HTC Products, Inc.

Introduction

For many craftsmen, woodworking is a way of creating something special, and for others, it is simply a means of escaping the pressures of the work week. For whatever reason, the workshop is a self-made environment in which to have fun and to build something.

The workshop is the place where you will discover the joys of woodworking. There you will learn many new skills as you familiarize yourself with the vast array of general purpose and specialized tools. There, too, you will begin to learn the vocabulary of woodworking.

The workshop presents an opportunity to make a seemingly endless variety of projects. You may start out making a few bookshelves and end up carving duck decoys, making toys, building chests of drawers, or turning decorative bowls. The properly designed woodworking workshop will provide you with a lifetime of enjoyment.

In this book, I have attempted to document a variety of workshops and different approaches to designing one. However, your space requirements, degree of interest, skill level, etc., are all factors that will determine the workshop environment you create for yourself. For example, not everyone will be interested in production work, nor be able to afford thousands of dollars to set up a shop. By reading about the variety of workshops in the following pages, you may discover one best suited for you.

Perception is undoubtedly the single most important concept related to planning and designing a shop. Unfortunately, there are many preconceived notions about what the workshop should be. Woodworkers are conditioned by other woodworkers, books, and television to believe that there is an ideal workshop for every purpose and that there is only one right way to set up a workshop. Nothing could be farther from the truth.

Many woodworkers consider the workshops shown in museums models of what the ideal workshop should be like. While the historical perspective of the workshop is useful, it is important to remember that museum workshops are representations of a work environment. Their primary purpose is to show the typical tools used by tradesmen at that period of time, not to accurately represent the organization and layout of an individual's shop.

Many photographs of contemporary shops also misrepresent the typical workshop. All the tools and materials are neatly arranged, there is no dust on the floors, bench, or machine surfaces, the safety guards are correctly positioned, and lighting is enhanced. In actuality, clamps, glue, chisels and other materials will be scattered about in a typical workshop. How comfortable and practical would the shop displayed in the photographs really be in an actual woodworking situation? Are those perfect storage units really accessible? Can you swing a long piece of wood without bashing light fixtures, the piece under construction, or the drill index sitting on the workbench?

The ideal workshop is one that reflects how you do your woodworking. If you build one piece at a time, then your shop has a definite cycle. In the beginning, the workshop is neat and tidy. As you build, dust, debris, tools, and other materials accumulate. When the piece is finished, then the shop is cleaned up and tools are put away. There might even be a period of inactivity—until the next project begins.

On the other hand, the shop which is in continuous use for the making of cabinets or picture frames has a different cycle. Wood, debris, tape measures, glue bottles and tools are probably always scattered about and ready for use. As chaotic as it might appear, these shops do have an order to them because of the dynamic flow of repeatable activity.

Woodworking shops, especially those at home, should be set up with as much planning and thought as possible. A shop haphazardly set up can eventually cause frustration and the complete abandonment of woodworking. The workshop has certain factors that must be approached in an organized fashion. Most people simply cannot have everything they desire in the shop, because floor and storage space is limited. Nor can most people afford much duplication. And, while you may dream of buying the most expensive and high-tech equipment, sometimes expensive items are not necessary.

Workshops are dynamic in that there is an ebb and flow of tools, machines, projects and material. The start-up shop may be sparse and equipped with tools that are essential. In contrast, the established shop is filled with an eclectic variety of tools which have proved to be useful.

The skill level of the woodworker will also affect how the workshop is designed. While a novice might be satisfied with sawhorses and an old door for a workbench, the seasoned woodworker will have long ago replaced it with a customized bench that better reflects his or her woodworking skills.

Many factors influence the design and use of a workshop. These factors vary in importance according to the woodworker's individual needs. One person may have 2,000 square feet of space for a workshop, but only be interested in making miniature carvings. Another person may have only 500 square feet and want to build four-poster bed frames.

You should first try to determine what area of woodworking you want to concentrate on. Some woodworkers want to specialize in a single type of work, whether it be lathe turning, chip carving, or scroll-saw projects. Other woodworkers have a general interest in many aspects of woodworking. Regardless of intention, it is still important to make your initial plans based upon need.

Therefore, the first step should be to make a list of your requirements according to the type of woodworking you plan on doing. Questions to consider: How much space do you have? Will this space be adequate in a year's time? Will the workshop be located in a garage, basement, or other building? Are 110- and 220-voltages available? Is the electrical wiring adequate for operating 10 to 15 amp motors? Is there an adequate number of AC outlets and are they properly located? Is the lighting and ventilation adequate? Are there entryways and storage facilities? Are the ceilings high enough? Do you have the proper heating, cooling, and humidity control? What machines and assorted tools are important? Can you get them into the shop, and will you be able to move safely and freely about them? Do you know the local zoning restrictions and have the proper insurance coverage? All these concerns are addressed in the following chapters.

There are two stories that illustrate the importance of planning when setting up a workshop. In the first, a person becomes passionately interested in woodworking. He decides to build a shop and do woodworking. He wants to build something simply for the personal satisfaction. He straightens up a corner of the basement and purchases a table saw, a router, and a few hand tools.

Things quickly begin to get complicated. On his first trip to the lumberyard, the woodworker encounters his first real problem: how to buy lumber and how to transport the lumber home. Somehow this is accomplished, and the miscellaneous pieces of solid lumber and plywood are squeezed into the basement. But our intrepid woodworker chooses not to organize the lumber. The rationale is that it will not matter if wood is leaned against the wall or stacked directly on the concrete floor, because the expectation is that work will begin immediately.

The table saw is plugged in and a trial cut made in a rough piece of oak. The cut is completed, but not before the overhead lights dim and smoke rises from the blade. The saw is rather noisy. The air is filled with dust and smoke.

Undeterred, our novice woodworker starts to build the most complex bookcase ever envisioned, but is stopped dead in his tracks because there are not enough tools, an adequate workbench, or sufficient space to rip a sheet of plywood. Frustration arises. Magazines and books are reviewed, and there are more visits to the local tool store.

The woodworker arms himself with new information and more tools, but finds this makes woodworking even more confusing. The attempt at building a bookcase is forgotten and new pursuits such as lathe turning and decoy carving are undertaken. The woodworker meanders from one project to another, continuing to redefine what type of woodworking interests him. In the end, the basement is filled with every imaginable tool and accessory, his bank account is depleted, and nothing has ever been made.

In the second scenario, someone who has attended a woodworking seminar becomes so taken by the charm and apparent ease of the demonstrator's skill that he cannot wait to do the same. This person has seen photographs of what a "real" workshop looks like and has decided to duplicate a professional's shop for himself. He visits the bank and secures a substantial loan. Instead of using a garage or basement, he builds a separate structure next to his house. The new workshop is complete with 110- and 220-volt wiring, heating, cooling, humidity control, a central dust-collection system, a spray-painting room and lumber-storage racks. Next, he purchases everything that a shop requires: production-quality table saws, wide-bed jointers, deep-throat band saws, stroke sanders, assorted routers and every imaginable hand tool and accessory.

Afterward, our woodworker attends every seminar and workshop in the country and buys every book about woodworking. He continues to buy the newest tools and the most expensive antique hand tools, and stockpiles rare and exotic hardwoods. This person has an appetite that cannot be satisfied. But he still has not made any-

thing, and his family wonders if the promised objects will ever be built.

Many woodworkers have become like the woodworkers described in these examples. That is why it is so important to *define* your woodworking interests and plan out your workshop carefully. In the following chapters you will learn how to design a workshop best suited to your individual needs.

CHAPTER ONE

Designing a Space

A master chairmaker once said that it is difficult to know if a chair is comfortable until you sit in it. The same principle applies to arranging a workshop; it is difficult to know if a particular layout is useful until the workshop has been used. There is no ideal way of laying out the tools, ventilation system, storage area, etc., because each shop is different.

Many books and magazines describe specific shop layouts. This is disadvantageous because it restricts layout to one or two workshops and does not delve into the process that consists of working within the parameters such as shop size and budget.

Rather than describe specific layout plans, it is more helpful to deal with layout by describing how to cope with problems that may be encountered. This is because the workshop will evolve and change according to the needs of the woodworker.

Most woodworkers start off with a space, make an educated guess as to requirements, and begin the setup. As we gain more woodworking experience and expand the amount of equipment needed in the workshop, we rearrange the workshop and create a plan for future needs and requirements.

Workshops do have certain commonalities like machines, ventilation, electricity and storage. However, there are also many differences in individual circumstances. Consider two garages: one in Florida and another in Wisconsin. The obvious differences in the seasons will affect the design and use of the workshops. Or, consider two people who each have identical spaces in which to set up a workshop. One, however, has an unlimited budget and the other is tightly budgeted. The one with the unlimited budget will not be restrained from purchasing any tool, machine, or accessory. However, this doesn't mean that his workshop is better than a frugally set up workshop.

The factors that control shop layout are usually more limiting than expansive. The list of constraints can include the following:

1. Shop location. Will the shop be located in the garage, basement, shed, a room in the house, or an off-site location?
2. Size of shop. What is the square footage, wall lengths, and floor-to-ceiling height of the workshop?
3. Shop configuration. Is it square, rectangle, L or T shape, etc?
4. Finances. How much do you plan to spend on tools, materials, lighting, heating, cooling, ventilation, and storage?
5. Type of work. Do you plan to carve, turn, build furniture, do restoration work or marquetry, or make instruments, miniatures, toys, gun stocks, or birdhouses?
6. Special requirements. How will you deal with heating, cooling, humidity control, sound insulation, and security?

Start designing a workshop layout by making a list of the tools, materials, hardware, and supplies that you feel will be used in the shop. This list should include both current and future needs. When making the list, group similar items together, such as hand tools, painting supplies, or nuts and bolts.

Before developing a floor plan, consider the requirements pertaining to tools, storage, and open space. For example, radial arm saws are usually placed against a wall and table saws customarily have space on all four sides. Drill presses, shapers, jointers and planers need space on three sides and can be placed near walls. Paints and finishing supplies are best stored independently of other items and should be kept away from heat sources in a dust-free cabinet. Workbenches can be against a wall or open on four sides. There should be sufficient working

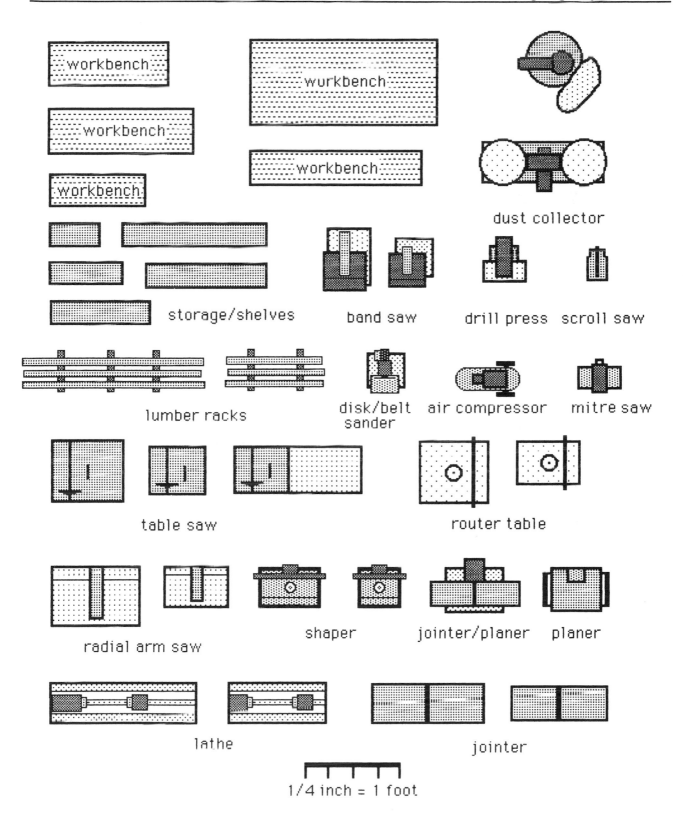

Illus. 1-1. Tool symbols used for workshop layout.

area around the front and sides of the workbench and table saw. If tools are equipped with mobile bases, their storage area should be reasonably open.

Measure the floor space of the proposed work area. Include all windows, doors, and other obstructions. Draw a sketch of the floor plan using the architectural scale of ¼ inch equals 1 foot. Use a copy machine to reproduce Illus. 1-1 (scale: ¼ inch to 1 foot), and cut out the appropriate tool representations. Move these templates around on the floor plan.

Analyze your own work habits and the sequence of operations that normally apply to shop work. In Illus. 1-2, the machines are oriented to take advantage of the large door opening. For instance, as lumber is brought into the shop, the first stop might be at the radial arm saw or circular saw accompanied by sawhorses. The lumber is then moved to the workbench, jointer/planer, or to storage. As you are working at the workbench, you may make repeated trips to the table saw, or router table, or a cabinet of hand tools. It would be convenient to locate storage units near the associated tools, such as drill bit storage near the drill press, hand tools near the workbench and clamps near the assembly area (Illus. 1-3). Rearrange the tool templates in the floor plan as you think through the work process.

When the templates are arranged in a satisfactory manner, make several permanent drawings of the floor plan. Use the copies to position pipes and hose locations for the dust-collection system, electrical wiring and outlets, and lighting. (Refer to the chapters on dust-collection systems and electrical wiring for additional information.) You now have a layout of your workshop.

Illus. 1-2. The table saw, jointer, and planer are positioned in alignment with the large door opening to make it easier to work with long boards. The open space to the left of the jointer is in front of a workbench.

Illus. 1-3. Storage units are placed near the machines. The wall cabinet with drill bits is to the right of the drill press. Lathe tools are positioned above the lathe. The portable air compressor is moved when either the lathe or drill press is used. The small bench has a machinist's vise and a metal tool box.

CHAPTER TWO
Power and Lights

Unless you are fortunate enough to have an industrial building for a workshop, or you only intend to work with hand tools or electrical tools that have low power requirements, you will have to consider ways to provide adequate power for your shop. Most homes built in the United States within the last 40 or 50 years have two 120-volt power lines and a ground wire that runs from the electric meter to a service panel. The 120-volt lines are used in branch circuits and provide the power to operate lights and most appliances. To power appliances such as ranges and clothes driers, which require more power, the pair of 120-volt wires are combined to make 240 volts. Some older homes which have only a single 120-volt wire and ground wire entering the service panel lack the capability to provide 240 volts.

The workshop obviously uses electrical power, but in a different way than the home. In the home, it's not unusual for the refrigerator, oven, dehumidifier, washing machine, radio, television, VCR, lights, and door bell to be operating at the same time.

It's a different situation in the shop. The one-person shop will probably have only a few electrical items, such as lights, a machine and a dust collector, operating at the same time. In the shop, it would be unusual to be operating a band saw at the same time the table saw is in use. Not only is this dangerous, but it's a waste of electricity. And if the shop is underwired, having two electrical motors operating at the same time places an overload on both the electrical system and the machines' motors.

Even though few machines and tools are in operation at one time, the shop has to be sufficiently equipped to handle the electrical needs of all machines—both current and future. Your machines and the way you work are going to define your electrical requirements. In a general-purpose workshop, a table saw (1–3-horsepower motor), dust collector (1–2-horsepower motor), and router (1–5-horsepower motor) are typical machines. Compare the power requirements of this shop to a carver's workshop which uses a Dremel Moto-Tool (1 amp), a 3/8-inch drill (3.5 amps), and a finish sander (2 amps).

As shown in Illus. 2-1, most electric motors are labelled as to the horsepower value at specific voltage and amps. However, the term horsepower can be confusing, because it is frequently used as an indicator of the powerfulness of a machine. Horsepower is used to describe everything from lawnmowers and cars to routers and table saws. But does the indicated horsepower represent motor power when the motor is first turned on, or does it indicate the power while the motor is running? (According to the

Illus. 2-1. A Leeson ½-horsepower, 8.8 amp, 115v or 4.4, 208/230v motor.

encyclopedia, one mechanical horsepower is equivalent to 33,000 foot-pounds of work per minute. Electric horsepower is determined from the electrical input in watts minus any loss due to heat and friction of the motor itself. One mechanical horsepower is equal to 746 watts.)

A more preferable and simpler method of determining your electrical requirements is to disregard horsepower entirely and instead use amperes, or "amps," as the primary indicator of machine power. An amp is a unit of electric current equivalent to a steady current produced by one volt applied across a resistance of one ohm. Amps are easy to use because electrical fuses, circuits, and most electrical devices are rated in amps. It's more straightforward to check amps, rather than horsepower, to determine whether a tool can be used in your electrical system.

Workshop motors, especially motors that are exposed to sawdust, should be totally enclosed with an internal fan for cooling and a reset button. Motors are safer and more efficient if they are sealed against dust and operate at lower temperatures. The reset button acts like a circuit breaker to shut the motor off if the electrical supply is insufficient. If the line amperage is too low for the motor to operate correctly, the motor may start up but will shut off as it overheats. When the motor cools down, the reset button can be pushed to restart the motor.

The most common symptoms of an overloaded system are quickly discovered in the workshop. If the lights dim, the machine motor stops, or a fuse or circuit blows whenever a motor is turned on, check the line voltage and amperage—especially if this situation happens repeatedly. Also check your electrical system to be sure the circuit panel and AC outlet are properly grounded. If not, they should be.

If you are setting up a shop, start by making a list of all the electrical tools, lights, fans, heaters, humidifiers, and dehumidifiers that will be installed. Determine the voltage and the amperage of each item, and make a best guess as to which will be operating at the same time.

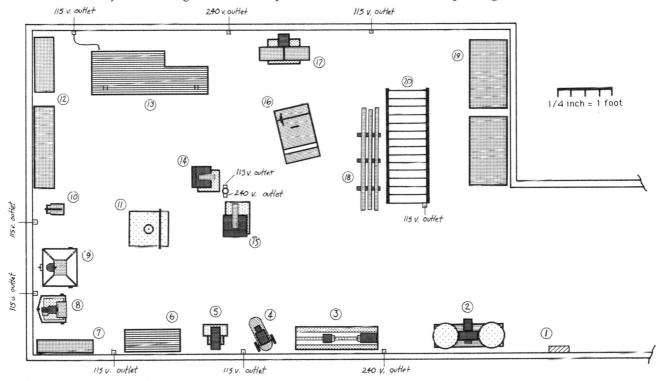

Illus. 2-2. Shop layout and electrical outlet location: 1, electrical subpanel for workshop; 2, dust collector; 3, lathe; 4, air compressor; 5, drill press; 6, workbench; 7, shelf storage; 8, disc/belt sander on mobile base; 9, router joinery machine on mobile base; 10, scroll saw; 11, router table; 12, tool storage; 13, workbench; 14, small band saw; 15, large band saw; 16, table saw; 17, jointer/planer; 18, lumber storage; 19, wood storage; 20, stairs to upper floor. Note: The workbench (13) has outlet strips mounted to each front leg.

Next, decide where the stationary machines will be located and draw a layout of the shop. Indicate in your layout the position of all electrical outlets. The outlets should be spread throughout the shop on all four walls and the ceiling. Be sure to plan for extra outlets in areas where there might be future need. Then decide upon the outlet height from the floor.

At this point you are ready to either hire an electrician or install the wiring yourself. If you plan to install your own wiring, remember that electricity is potentially dangerous, especially if you aren't sure of the basics of wiring and electrical safety procedures. Check with your local city or county planning office and obtain a work permit if it is required. If you haven't had any previous experience working with electricity, borrow reference books from your local library to learn as much as you can about safety, tools, wiring and electrical fixtures before beginning the job.

Before you start the actual work, make a shopping list of tools and all wiring needs. Then go to an electrical supply store to determine costs. There are specialized tools and testing equipment which are needed for installation, and a diversity of wire types and gauges, couplings, conduits, receptacles, fuses, circuit breakers and fittings from which to select. Before buying, you may want to call an electrician for an estimate. The cost for the estimate is usually low, and you might be surprised to discover how reasonable the cost for the job is. Remember, both you and the electrician have to purchase parts, so the principal difference is tools, labor and skill.

My own preference was to get the shop operational as quickly as possible so that I could begin using my shop to make furniture. I hired a certified electrician who knew the local codes and had the correct equipment and supplies.

Electrical Subpanel

For my shop, I had the electrician install a subpanel directly off the main circuit-breaker panel, as shown in Illus. 2-3. A subpanel offers several advantages. The shop's electrical system is independent of the electrical system for the house, and can be shut off separately. I can even lock the subpanel, if additional security is required. The subpanel shown in Illus. 2-3 is wired so that I have both 110- and 220-volt service in the shop. It also has separate circuits for individual machines, lights, and specific outlets.

If your existing main service panel has the capacity, and there are circuit-breaker slots or fuse blocks available, it's possible to have the shop wired directly from the main service panel. However, you may find that you are working at the very limits of the electrical capacity of the system, which may restrict the number of tools which can be operational at one time, as well as future tool use.

Wall Outlets

It's simple to customize AC (alternate current) wall outlets for the shop. For example, one half of a duplex

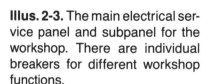

Illus. 2-3. The main electrical service panel and subpanel for the workshop. There are individual breakers for different workshop functions.

outlet box can be wired for 10 amps and the other half wired for 15 amps (or if you choose, 15 amps and 20 amps). Simply color-code the outlets by using white or black receptacles. This makes it easy to visually identify outlets for specific tools and to separate wall outlets to be used for either stationary or portable tools. This system is also more economical because you are not using a 20-amp circuit for a tool which only requires 5 amps.

AC outlets should be placed in convenient locations. It's a nuisance to have only a few outlets hidden in hard-to-reach locations. It's also not wise to rely on extension cords indefinitely because they are potential tripping hazards. Long extension cords can also cause tools to overheat due to lost amps. As a general rule, extension cords should be used sparingly and only for portable hand tools.

Lighting

First, no matter what type and how many light fixtures there are in the shop, wire the lights on their own dedicated circuit. This provides a safety factor because you can turn the machines off at the circuit breaker to maintain them or for emergencies without turning off the lights. And if there is an overload condition and a machine blows a fuse or circuit, the lights will stay on.

There are two principal types of lighting: incandescent and fluorescent. Incandescent light, while adequate for household lighting, isn't generally acceptable in workshops. The "bare bulb" light isn't bright enough to light large work areas. The light is from a single point, and you have to work directly under the light bulb to have adequate light. If you work at random locations in the shop, then this would mean having a bulb for every square foot of work space.

Incandescent lights are satisfactory for shop applications that require a bright, focused light source in order for detail work to be visible. Carving, turning, inlay and marquetry are some woodworking applications that benefit from a single-light source. Often, a goose-neck lamp is positioned near the work so that it can be adjusted to the work at hand. However, a single-light source should not be used as a substitute for general room lighting; rather, it should be used to augment existing light levels.

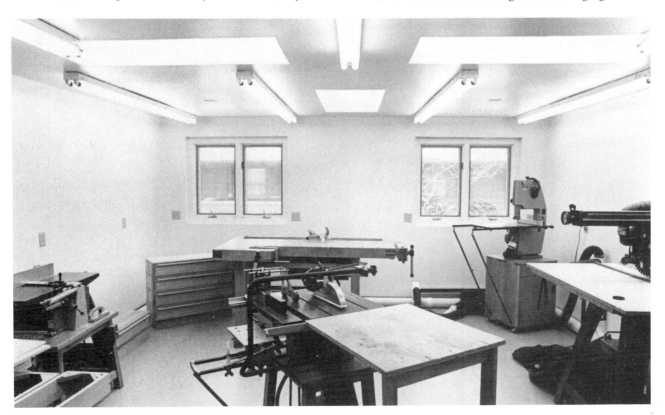

Illus. 2-4. This 18 × 18-foot workshop has windows, skylights, 8-foot fluorescent lights, and wall and ceiling AC receptacles.

Most workshops rely on fluorescent lights as the principal source of illumination. Fluorescent lights offer a low profile and good overall lighting for most shops. They are easy to install against flat ceilings, and between or mounted to joists. The most common fixtures are available, as either single or double lights, in lengths of 4 and 8 feet in cool or warm tones. Because of the extended length of the light source, light is spread evenly over the work area. Fluorescent lights are becoming more energy-efficient and are certainly worth considering as replacements for older lights.

If you are painting new pieces or reproducing colors on an antique restoration, then your light source should be "color-balanced." The best source of color-balanced light is sunlight, so paint near a window if possible. If this isn't feasible, then combine different light sources, that is, warm and cool lights or incandescent and fluorescent lights, to approximate daylight. A commercial art supply or paint store may suggest other lighting solutions.

Bill Daley, a woodworker, integrated double 8-foot fluorescent units with windows, skylights, and white walls and ceiling to create a bright and shadowless work environment in his workshop. AC outlets are spaced evenly around the walls at a height of 3½ feet and on the ceiling (Illus. 2-4).

One disadvantage of fluorescent lights is that the tube can be accidentally broken when you are moving long boards. However, the tubes can be protected in several ways. The most expensive way is to buy fixtures with built-in plastic diffusion screens. Two other alternatives, which work with the open metal-shade or plain-fixture styles, are covering the fixture with plastic or metal screening or installing clear plastic sleeves on the fluorescent lights (Illus. 2-5). The sleeves encase the entire light, including the ends, so that the glass fragments remain within the plastic sleeve if the light breaks.

Sometimes a well-lit room doesn't provide adequate light for carving. Diffuse overhead light is like sunshine at noon; it falls directly down upon an object and creates no shadows. This is disadvantageous when you are working on relief carvings or chip carvings, because shadows help define the work area. Dick Dermody, a woodcarver, solved this problem by mounting a bright halogen lamp head on a portable stand next to the workbench. He can easily adjust the lamp to create side lighting for a carving piece (Illus. 2-6).

Workbench Outlets

The workbench is probably the most common location

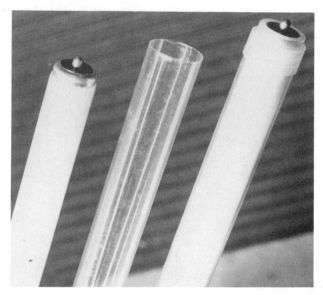

Illus. 2-5. A fluorescent light tube and clear protective sleeve and end caps.

Illus. 2-6. This work area has a halogen lamp for side lighting to give more detail to carving relief work.

for using hand-held power tools. Unfortunately, the bench is not a convenient place for cords and AC outlets. Cords are bothersome when you have assorted tools and lumber on the bench top.

Let's consider several locations where outlets could be mounted on the workbench: the front, rear, floor, and sides. If the outlet is mounted at the front edge, it can interfere with clamping and assembly work. If the outlet is mounted at the rear, the cord will drape across the bench top and whatever else is there. Mounting the outlet near the floor is better, because heavy-duty extension cords could be used anywhere at the bench. But there will always be a tangle of cords at your feet. The sides are the ideal location for permanently installing AC outlets.

I installed outlet strips on each of the front bench legs, as shown in Illus. 2-7. The strips installed, Power Master Model EP-6S, by Waber Inc., have six receptacles, surge

and noise suppression, a rating of 15 amps continuous duty, and an illuminated on/off switch and reset button. This provides me with an outlet location that is easy to reach and doesn't clutter the bench top or floor. Note from Illus. 2-7 that electrical tie wraps are used to secure the power cord and keep it out of the way.

Special Accessories

The Automater from R. F. St. Louis Associates is a new product that is very handy for operating a power tool in conjunction with a dust collector or vacuum. The Automater (Illus. 2-8–2-10) can be used to automatically turn on a dust collector or vacuum whenever a sander, band saw, or table saw is switched on. The model DC-1200 Automater is 120 volts and has two AC receptacles in the front and a standard plug in the rear. The model DC-2500 is also 120 volts, but is mounted on an extension cord.

To use the Automater, simply plug it into the AC outlet. The receptacle labelled "control outlet" is for the power tool. The receptacle labelled "switched outlet" is for the dust collector or vacuum. After the power tool is

Illus. 2-7. A Waber, Inc. Power Master outlet strip mounted to the workbench leg.

Illus. 2-8. The model DC-1200 Automater.

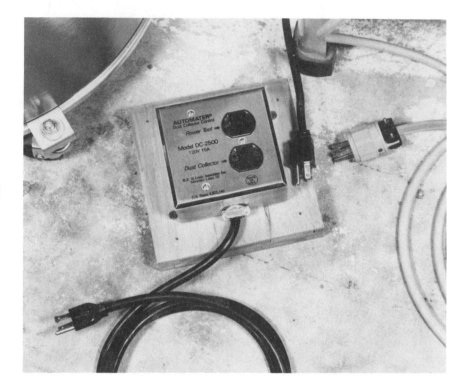

Illus. 2-9. The model DC-2500 Automater.

Illus. 2-10. The model DC-2400 Automater.

switched on, the dust collector or vacuum is automatically switched on. When the tool is switched off, the dust collector or vacuum is automatically switched off.

The model DC-1200 Automater can be used with dust collectors rated at 8 amps, with a combined power requirement for both tools and dust collector of 15 amps.

Model DC-2500 Automater can be used with dust collectors rated at 15 amps. The model DC-2400 Automater is a 220-volt version that is installed in the electrical box. It is designed for dust collectors rated at 16 amps in combination with another power tool as long as the total power requirement is less than 20 amps. The Automater is particularly useful when you are operating tools, such as a plate joiner, that are repeatedly switched on and off for quick successive cuts.

A small, but absolutely essential, item for any electrical tool is the AC plug. Many modern tools are double-grounded and don't have plugs with a ground pin. This type of AC plug is small, moulded, and extremely durable. However, if you change AC cords or need to replace the plug, visit an electrical supply store and purchase hospital-grade plugs (Illus. 2-11). These plugs are made by a number of manufacturers and are easily identified by their labels and a green dot. The hospital-grade plug has heavy-duty AC blades and recessed plug assembly screws. It is designed to withstand the physical abuses caused by feet and heavy beds that roll. This is advantageous in the workshop, where there are mobile tool bases, the possibility of falling lumber, and where plugs are occasionally roughly yanked from outlets.

The twist-lock AC plug is also noteworthy. I have installed these on all my stationary machines. The plug

Illus. 2-11. Hospital-grade plugs by different manufacturers. Note that the plugs are identified with labels and green dots.

Illus. 2-12. The Hubbell model No. 4570-C twist-lock plug, and receptacle.

blades can only be inserted by twisting the plug as it enters the outlet receptacle. Once it is in place, it is very secure and can only be removed by twisting it in the opposite direction. These are also very useful when you are installing AC outlets on ceilings. They won't fall out and can't accidentally be pulled from the outlet (Illus. 2-12).

Because of consumer interest in conservation and energy savings, high-efficiency motors are being used in some woodworking machines. Most high-efficiency motors require three-phase electrical power, and are more efficient if the motor is used continuously, as in some commercial environments. At this time, there are only a few single-phase high-efficiency motors available, and they tend to be more expensive than the equivalent standard motor. For the small shop which infrequently uses a motor in a continuous manner, there is minimal benefit to switching to high-efficiency motors at present.

CHAPTER THREE

Storage

Storage is a necessary requirement of any shop, but it is something woodworkers rarely consider until the last moment. Usually, we are so interested in setting up the shop to build things, that we will use almost anything for storage. Unfortunately, once a poor storage system is installed, it's often difficult to ever be rid of it.

Hand tools, power tools, lumber, and finishing supplies all have different storage requirements (for both the

Illus. 3-1. Freestanding tool cabinets. Note the large work area in front of the workbench and easy access to stored tools.

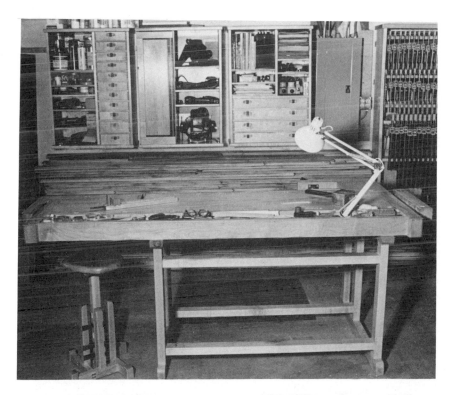

Illus. 3-2. Wall-hung tool cabinets. There is a 4-foot-wide standing/working area between workbench cabinets.

Illus. 3-3. Tool storage has been integrated into this freestanding workbench.

present and future). Pay attention to these four simple rules when considering storage space:

1. The storage system has to be designed and built for your own specific needs.
2. Planning and building a storage system takes time and materials.
3. The storage system should be compact enough to be out of the way, yet accessible when you are working.
4. The storage system should be adequate for expanding tool collections.

Three different approaches to tool storage in relationship to the workbench are shown in Illus. 3-1–3-3. The first system is based upon floor-standing cabinets, the next upon wall-hung cabinets, and the third on storage integrated into a bench. Each system is very efficient and works well for its respective users.

Keep in mind future plans for the workshop when determining which type of storage system to use. If, for example, a wall storage system is designed as a single large unit and is anchored to a concrete wall, then the storage unit is either left with the house or broken apart for transport when it is necessary to move to a new location. On the other hand, if three freestanding units were built to use the same space, they could be moved with relative ease. Every floor plan is different, so a large storage unit may not fit into a new location, and new storage units will need to be constructed.

Jon Arno, a woodworker, solved the problem of being able to relocate his workshop easily by constructing a number of vertical drawer "columns" which are used to support bench tops of different lengths (Illus. 3-4). Each drawer system is freestanding and can be placed just about anywhere. The bench top has a series of drawers set back from the front edge, and the top unit is simply placed upon the drawer columns. The top unit is heavy and the back edge is usually positioned against a wall, so it does not slide on the drawer columns. If the bench top is extra long, it can be supported with a center brace. Construction-grade plywood and pine and fir are used throughout the storage system. These woods are inexpensive and readily available in most cities. One other notable feature of this system is that the units are constructed

Illus. 3-4. This tool storage workbench is positioned against the wall.

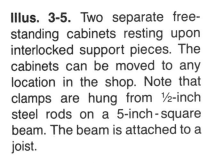

Illus. 3-5. Two separate free-standing cabinets resting upon interlocked support pieces. The cabinets can be moved to any location in the shop. Note that clamps are hung from ½-inch steel rods on a 5-inch-square beam. The beam is attached to a joist.

so that their heights are all the same and just slightly lower than the top of the table saw. In a small shop this allows wood to be easily supported from any location.

I have moved three times in the past 13 years and this has affected my method of storage. My wife and I rented our first house in Southern California, and my workshop was in the garage. Not only was the garage small, but it was also used for the automobile and yard tools. This meant that the storage units and machinery had to be as unobtrusive as possible. At that time, I purchased tools that could be easily moved onto the driveway so that I could work out of doors. (The lightweight table saw and band saw were made mainly of aluminum with wooden stands. An added advantage of these tools was that they would not rust in the salty oceanic air of Santa Monica. This also proved to be an advantage when we moved to Milwaukee and into a house with a small, damp basement.)

The storage cabinet I built for the California garage was made of oak plywood, and it measured 18 inches deep × 43 inches wide by 72 inches tall, with an 8-inch base to keep the cabinet well away from floor moisture (Illus. 3-5). The unit was composed of 12 shelves, six of which were behind a door. The cabinet sat freely upon a base composed of interlocking feet and supports. Another open cabinet was made at a later time to help organize a growing tool collection. The units were easy to move and could be placed anywhere within the shop.

Since I like to have tools close to the work area, all of the tools were near the end of the workbench.

Another tool storage area is shown in Illus. 3-6. This system is composed of three different units: a commer-

Illus. 3-6. This storage system is comprised of a commercially made tool chest, a narrow drawer chest found at a flea market, and an open plywood cabinet.

Illus. 3-7. The drawer in this tool chest has tongue-and-groove dividers to separate small planes.

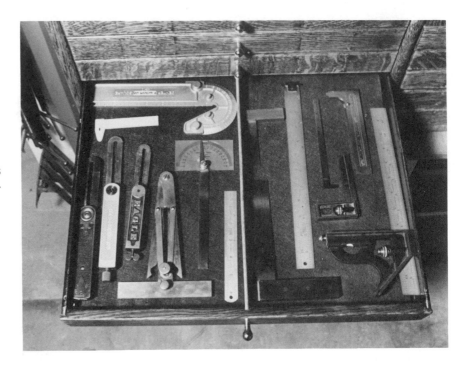

Illus. 3-8. The narrow drawer is lined with felt and filled with measuring tools.

cially made tool chest, a shallow drawer chest discovered at a swap meet, and a plywood cabinet with several shelves. Chisels, planes, layout tools, speciality hammers, router guide bushes, putty knives, and other smaller tools are stored in the first two units (Illus. 3-7 and 3-8). The bottom unit is for storing items I do not need to reach quickly. Here, I keep plastic airtight jars of dowels and biscuit plates, and seldom-used tools. The plastic jars (Illus. 3-9) prevent the sealed-up wooden pieces from swelling due to atmospheric moisture, so they retain their original size and will fit dowel holes and plate joinery slots correctly. Because the jars are see-through, it is very

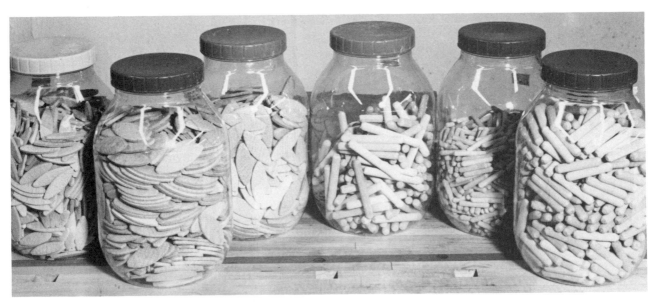

Illus. 3-9. Large plastic jars are excellent for storing dowels and biscuit plates because the contents are visible, clean, and dry.

apparent when the contents need to be resupplied. I found the jars (which were very inexpensive) in the houseware section of a department store. Also note the post which holds an assortment of clamps.

Another storage location is the overhead rafters or ceiling joists. I am not fond of storing heavy lumber or other cumbersome items in the rafters, because of the danger to myself and potential damage to tools and workpieces under construction if a long board is dropped or bangs against something as it is removed. If rafters are easy to get to and not part of the shop environment, they are good for drying green or wet wood. But be certain the framework can support the load of wood. I do hang jigs and templates on joists where they meet the wall. This is also a good location for hanging cabinets or other storage units (Illus. 3-10–3-13).

Shelving is probably the most common type of shop storage, especially when a shop is first set up. Typically, steel shelf units or wood shelves resting on metal brackets are used. With time, these shelves begin to wobble, lean, and sag because of the size or weight of the woodworking equipment stored on them. The other problem associated with shelving is one of access. Shelves that are too high become a refuse for clutter and dust. Shelves that are too low are difficult to use. And shelving that is too deep will become a haven for forgotten tools and supplies.

There are several commercial shelving systems designed to fit a variety of locations and requirements. One of these is Saturday's Solutions from Pacific Pine. It is a system of upright standards, shelves, drawers, bench tops, doors and fittings which are easy to assemble and can be positioned in most locations. The basic modular unit measures 18 × 35 inches. For longer units, additional 18 × 35-inch units can be attached so that a complete wall unit can be constructed (Illus. 3-13 and 3-14).

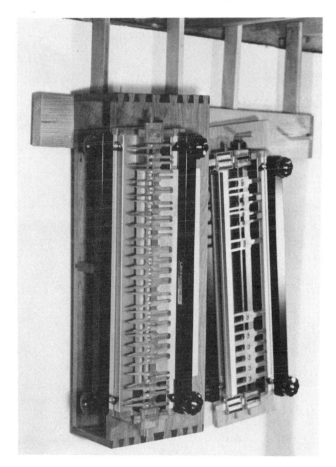

Illus. 3-10. A clamp storage unit suspended from joists. The hanger board is made of 1 × 4½ × 70-inch maple with ½ × 8-inch steel-rod clamp hangers.

Illus. 3-11. Leigh Industries dovetail and multiple mortise jigs hung on a joist-suspended hanger board.

Illus. 3-12. Various handsaws neatly stored on this joist-suspended storage unit.

Illus. 3-13 (above left). Saturday's Solution (Tyee Forest Products, Co.) modular shelf, drawer, and workbench units. Illus. 3-14 (above right). Saturday's Solution storage unit (Tyee Forest Products, Co.).

Monty Parker, a woodworker, does not use open shelving in his shop. Instead, the workshop walls are covered from floor to ceiling with pegboard (Illus. 3-15). The ⁓board is ¼-inch thick and supports a wide range of tools and accessories. There are a few kitchen-type cabinets, both at eye level and below the bench tops, for storing less used accessories (Illus. 3-16).

The principal work done in Monty Parker's shop is

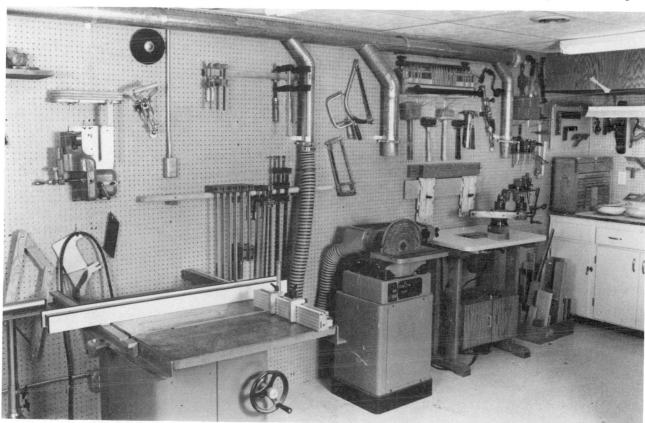

Illus. 3-15. Floor-to-ceiling pegboard storage.

Illus. 3-16. Pegboard storage mounted above recycled kitchen cabinets.

lathe turning. Consequently, the lathe is placed near a wall so that all of the tools and accessories are easily reached (Illus. 3-17). Two types of lathe tool holders are shown: a magnetic bar and a slotted board. Of the two styles, the magnetic bar (Illus. 3-18) is less favored because it magnetizes the tools.

Illus. 3-17. The lathe work area surrounded by pegboard-stored turning accessories.

Illus. 3-18. Lathe tools suspended from a magnetic bar mounted to pegboard.

Other frequently used tools have their own specialized location and storage. Various tool rests are inserted into holes drilled into a mounted board (Illus. 3-19). Sandpaper is stored by type and grit size in plastic bins which were purchased at a home improvement hardware store. These bins lend themselves to storage of a range of small items, including screws, hinges, toy parts and electrical fittings.

Clamps are stored by simply tightening them on a vertical wood strip or are hung suspended from a hori-zontal 1¼-inch by 5-foot wood dowel (Illus. 3-20 and 3-21). Other accessories are simply suspended from the pegboard nearest the principal tool, such as the mitre guide next to the table saw, or planes and squares near the workbench. Since the lathe-turned pieces are finished while still on the lathe, the Forcdom power tool with small sanding disc is suspended from the ceiling framework directly over the lathe (Illus. 3-22).

By necessity, the small shop must be space-efficient. One way to ensure this is to use the areas beneath open-

Illus. 3-19. Small plastic bins used to store various grades of sandpaper for lathe-turning work. Tool rests are stored in a wood strip. Holes were drilled at a slight angle, and the tool rest post simply fits into the holes.

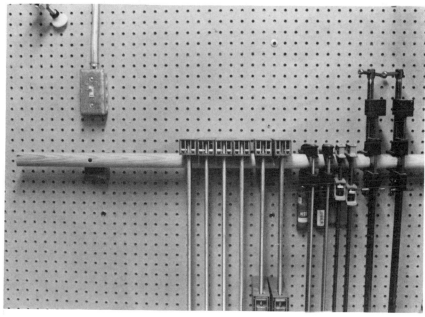

Illus. 3-20. The clamps are suspended from a large dowel rod that is mounted to the pegboard.

framed or bench-top machines. As shown in Illus. 3-23 and 3-24, cabinets with either drawers or slide-out shelves are ideal for bench-top drill presses. This type of cabinet needs to be stable and of adequate size. The storage unit with the drawers provides more than enough storage for drill bits, sanding drums, and other miscellaneous accessories for the drill press. The shelf-storage unit uses metal drawer slides so that the shelf slides out and provides full use as well as clear visibility of the stored accessories.

Illus. 3-21. Wooden clamps are clamped to a vertical wood strip mounted to the pegboard.

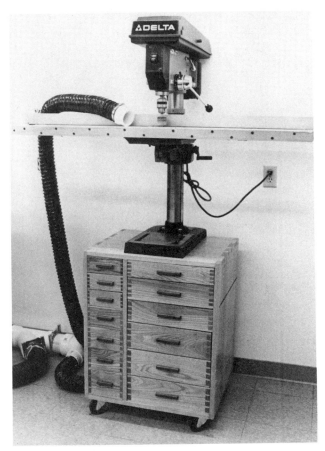

Illus. 3-23. The drill press is mounted to a small cabinet with lockable wheels. It features a custom-made table-and-fence system.

Illus. 3-22 (left). The Foredom power tool is suspended from a board mounted to the ceiling directly over the lathe, and is used for sanding work.

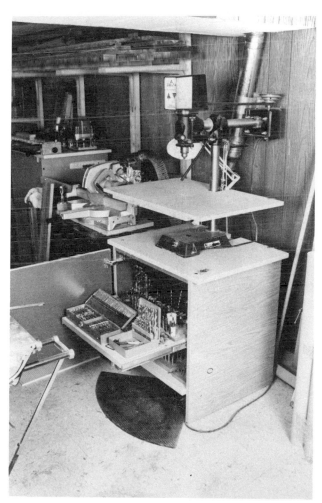

Illus. 3-24. The tabletop drill press mounted to a cabinet with shelves fitted with metal drawer slides.

Commercially made storage units for specific machines can also be used for space beneath a machine. The storage units in Illus. 3-25 and 3-26 are available from Sears to match its machines.

Some tools are designed in such a way that they present a storage problem. For example, just how should a router, tape measure, bottle of lubricating oil, chisel or awl be stored?

When I was setting up the router table for a project requiring finger joints, I first tried my setup by making several small trays. These trays turned out to be ideal for organizing small items for storage on a shelf (Illus. 3-27).

I keep files and rasps on the shelf below the small finger-jointed boxes. They rest in a 2-inch-wide dadoed board. This keeps them from banging into each other

and makes it easy for me to find and use different ones (Illus. 3-28).

Router bits are easy to store because their shafts provide a logical way for storage (Illus. 3-29). When drilling the holes for the router bit shafts, use a drill slightly larger than the diameter of the shaft. For example, if the shaft is ¼ inch, drill a ¹⁷/₆₄-inch hole. A simple stand with recessed locations is an ideal way to store routers with bits still attached. The center hole is large enough so that the bit easily fits, whether it's turning or not (Illus. 3-30).

Chisels are not simple to store, especially if you use them frequently. In the shops I visited, there seems to be three types of storage. Chisels are placed in drawers, suspended from a board with holes (or pegboard hangers), or kept randomly in a workbench tool tray. Storing chisels in a workbench tray is probably the worst of all possible solutions. Not only will the cutting edges be nicked or damaged, but you might eventually slice your fingers when reaching into the tray.

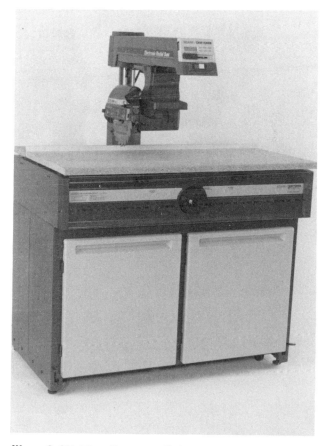

Illus. 3-25. The Sears radial arm saw with storage cabinet.

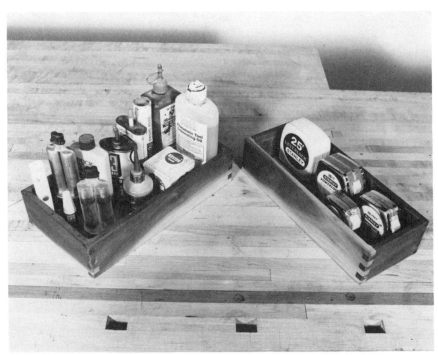

Illus. 3-26. The Sears lathe mounted to a cabinet with metal drawers.

Illus. 3-27. Small boxes made to store odds and ends. Making boxes is an ideal way to develop joinery techniques.

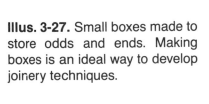

Illus. 3-28. A slotted strip of wood for storing files and rasps.

Illus. 3-29. Router bits that are stored in blocks of wood. The blocks are organized for different functions, that is, for dovetail jigs, large-diameter bits, and general-purpose bits.

Illus. 3-30. A router storage board with large openings.

There seems to be opposing theories for storing chisels in either a drawer or on a shelf-like board. I prefer the drawer system, because the chisels are isolated and removed from the workbench environment (Illus. 3-31). The only drawback is that the drawer must be specifically designed to accommodate the chisels. A second approach to drawer storage keeps the chisels isolated from each other and yet allows adequate space for fingers to grasp the handles (Illus. 3-32 and 3-33).

The one exception to drawer storage in my shop is a small cabinet to the right side of my bench (Illus. 3-34). It is located in an area away from the main work area, and I use it to store specialty tools such as carving tools, drawknives, and large mortising chisels.

Those who prefer to hang chisels from the wall do so because they want the chisels to be visible and easily accessible (Illus. 3-35). The choice of storage system for chisels seems to be related to how the workbench is used.

Illus. 3-31. Drawer-stored chisels. The chisels are separated by fixed wooden dividers.

Illus. 3-32. Drawer-stored chisels. The chisels rest upon wooden strips.

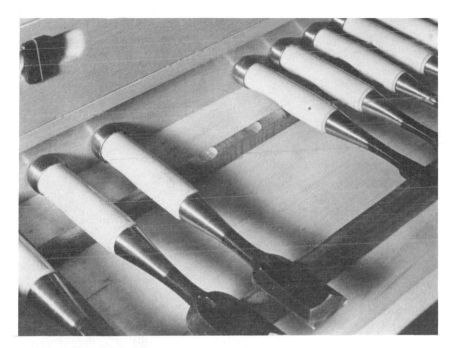

Illus. 3-33. Drawer-stored chisels. Note the notches for resting the chisel handles.

Illus. 3-34 (above left). A small storage cabinet with adjustable shelves for storing infrequently used tools. Illus. 3-35 (above right). Wall-hung chisels. The chisels fit through rectangular notches and rest upon their handles.

Chisels kept in drawers are mostly found with work-benches that are used on all four sides. Wall-hung chisels seem to be used with benches placed against a wall. In Illus. 3-36, note how the three small saws, two drawknives and numerous wooden moulding planes are stored.

Lathe tools should be stored close to the lathe. When designing a storage unit for lathe tools, make sure that it is large enough to accommodate future tools. Also design the unit so that the tools can be placed in any slot or holder, and are not restricted to a specific place. Illus. 3-37–3-39 show several variations of lathe tool holders.

Flea markets, swap meets, and yard sales can be sources for interesting and useful devices for storing tools. The 12-inch-diameter cobbler's nail tray shown in Illus. 3-40 is such an item. The tray rotates and the eight compartments are excellent for nails (of course), small tools, and parts for work in progress. Other finds from swap meets include the large table with a composition top and three drawers containing sliding trays, shown in Illus. 3-41 and 3-42. This was probably a machinist's bench. When searching at flea markets, always be on the lookout for small chests. Many of these provide good storage for smaller tools such as measuring devices and carving tools (Illus. 3-43).

The scroll-saw blade holder shown in Illus. 3-44 is made from two pieces of wood and has holes for specific blades. For ease of use, the blade sizes are permanently burned into the wood.

The clamp cabinet shown in Illus. 3-45 is built for a specific number and size of clamps. The "shelves" are

Illus. 3-36. Wall-hung chisels, marking and layout tools, and small hand saws.

Illus. 3-37. The lathe tools are mounted near the lathe. Note the sharpening grinder and small cardboard bins for storing sandpaper.

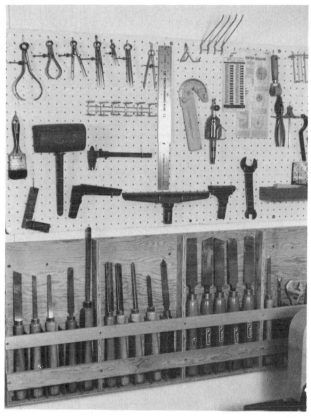

Illus. 3-38. Lathe tool storage and pegboard storage of accessories near the lathe.

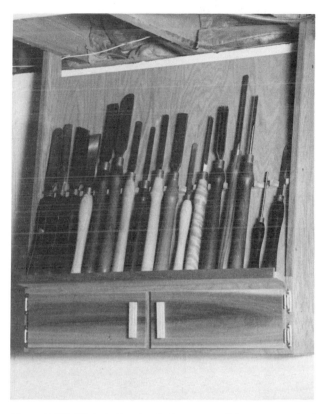

Illus. 3-39. This lathe-tool storage unit is suspended from joists. This unit has two small door compartments to keep the lathe parts clean.

Illus. 3-40. This shoemaker's Lazy Susan is useful for temporarily storing small items.

Illus. 3-41. A mechanic's bench with composition top and three drawers. Three commercially made tool boxes are used for smaller tools.

Illus. 3-42. There are sliding trays within the drawers of the mechanic's bench.

Illus. 3-43. This small chest found at a flea market is ideal for small tools.

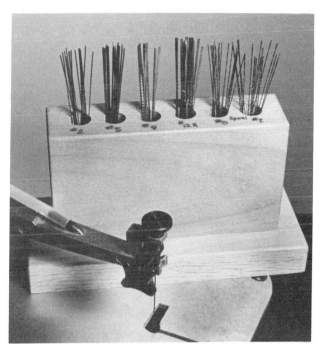

Illus. 3-44. Scroll-saw blades are stored in a block of wood, with identification numbers burned into the block.

Illus. 3-45. This wall-hung clamp storage unit is designed for a particular amount and size of clamps.

in specific locations so that the clamps can be clamped to them, and they also act as bumper boards for the clamp bars. The cabinet is made of maple with a plywood back, and is suspended on wooden hangers anchored to a concrete wall.

Lumber storage can be a major problem. Lumber requires a fair amount of floor or wall space, is heavy and awkward to move, and must be organized so that different woods can be found. Lumber stored directly upon the floor is susceptible to moisture, insects, worms, and small animals. Lumber stored in this way should rest upon thick pieces of wood to minimize the attack of moisture and pests. If the lumber is wet, place strips of wood between each layer of lumber.

For the small shop, a combination of floor and wall storage is most appropriate. This usually involves devising stout brackets or wall hangers. The lumber storage unit shown in Illus. 3-46 is composed of U-shaped metal channels. The pieces on the wall are attached with concrete anchors, and the horizontal pieces are bolted to the wall pieces so that they can be placed at any location. (The materials used are available from construction supply companies and are not expensive.) This design has several advantages over the typical pile of lumber on the floor. It is easy to see the stored material, the lumber is located away from floor moisture and most pests, and because the space capacity of a pair of brackets is limited, there is not a hefty pile of lumber to sort through. A sturdy wall and enough floor space for the brackets to project out about 2 feet are critical requirements of this design.

The low storage unit shown in Illus. 3-47 is made of construction 2 × 4's and is located in a small basement room adjacent to the workshop. The owner mostly makes lathe-turned objects and an occasional piece of furniture, so there is not a great demand for lumber stock. This

Illus. 3-46. Lumber stored on a wall-hung frame made of metal channel pieces. The channel pieces are purchased in lengths and then cut to size.

Illus. 3-47. A low storage rack for assorted lumber sizes.

Illus. 3-48. A floor-to-ceiling storage rack for assorted pieces of wood scraps and cutoff pieces accumulated after past work sessions and for other odds and ends.

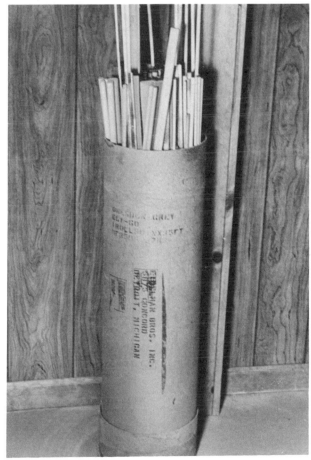

Illus. 3-49. This large shipping tube is useful for storing long dowels and other thin strips of wood.

means the lumber can be stored without being sorted by species and size.

The wood-framed storage unit shown in Illus. 3-48 is also made of 2 × 4's. It has plywood shelves and measures 32 inches deep, 57 inches wide, and 77 inches high, and was made to hold the odds and ends that accumulate after a work session, as well as short pieces and lathe blanks. Because it is located in a basement, it was designed to allow air to circulate around all surfaces to prevent moisture accumulation.

A large cardboard shipping tube approximately 8 inches in diameter × 30 inches in length is well suited for storing dowels and thin, long pieces of wood (Illus. 3-49).

Although I have focused primarily on tool storage, there are many other items in the workshop which need to be stored in an organized fashion. Sandpaper, sanding belts, hardware, paints and solvents, saw blades, and jigs

and fixtures all require storage. Some can be stored in a simple manner; for example, paint cans can be stored on shelves. Others, such as sanding belts or rotary tool bits, require a more creative solution. Sanding belts can be suspended on a large-diameter dowel mounted to ceiling joists (Illus. 3-50). Small carving bits, burs, and grinding points can be organized on shelves in a small cabinet (Illus. 3-51).

Make an inventory of your supplies and determine how to fit them in the open space of your shop. Solving the needs of storage requires practicality and ingenuity. The size and function of your workshop should be the first consideration in designing adequate storage. Try to keep similar tools grouped together and keep accessories near their primary tool. Keep in mind that any of the storage solutions shown can be modified to match your needs. Finally, plan for future needs and uses for the workshop.

Illus. 3-50. Sanding belts suspended from a joist-mounted dowel.

Illus. 3-51. The small sliding shelves and door on this cabinet are ideal for storing small carving and grinding bits and cutters.

CHAPTER FOUR
The Workbench

When I first became interested in woodworking, I was preoccupied with the need to select and buy power tools for the workshop. I was always reading magazine articles that described the first tools that should be bought for the workshop, but rarely were workbenches mentioned. As I began my first woodworking project, however, I realized that a solid, stable work surface was an absolute priority for building, carving, or even stacking workpieces (Illus. 4-1).

Workbenches can be classified in three broad groups: the simple workbench constructed of 2 × 4's and particle board, the factory-made bench, and the shop-made bench, which is custom-designed to suit one individual's style of woodworking. Each of these groups can be further differentiated according to utilization: the freestanding bench, the bench against a wall, and the bench with storage below the bench top (Illus. 4-2–4-4).

Simple Workbenches

The simple workbench of 2 × 4's and particle board is not the most effective workbench design. If constructed of standard framing 2 × 4's and nails, chances are the

Illus. 4-1. Seven-foot-long workbench with all sides accessible for work.

Illus. 4-2. Freestanding bench with large end vise.

Illus. 4-3. This workbench is located against the wall and can store tools. Note the metal pedestals supporting the workbench and the array of wooden planes.

Illus. 4-4. This workbench has storage space beneath the work surface.

bench will begin to wobble after a few uses. Construction with bolts or screws, while better, still can't take the twists and bows out of the 2 × 4's.

The flatness of particle board is dependent upon the flatness of the structure beneath it. Particle board attached to a 2 × 4 frame that isn't straight, flat, and true will also become warped. This may be acceptable when mixing paint and potting plants, but flat and true benches are an absolute necessity for most woodworking projects.

Particle board is principally used as a sheeting material for house construction. It was not designed to take surface abuse or absorb the vibrations from mallet and hammer blows which accompany carving and joinery work. And as the quality of work improves, this style of bench is typically replaced.

Factory-Made Workbenches

The factory-made bench, constructed of beech, maple and exotic woods, can be as beautiful as a fine piece of furniture. Many factory-made benches reflect the values of traditional joinery benches from our historic past, and their design is derived from a period when hand tools were primarily used. Bench vises and dogs are artifacts

from this period, when it was necessary to secure wood to a bench so that it could be planed, chiselled, and sawed by hand. Some benches have tool trays for storing hand tools while you are working, and others have drawers beneath the bench top. If you are considering a factory-made bench, be certain it reflects your style of woodworking. And be especially aware of the locations of the vises if you are left-handed. As beautiful and as practical as factory-made benches are, they are expensive.

The Ulmia Ultimate Workbench (Illus. 4-5), which is manufactured in Germany, is made of red beech and features a front and end vise with square-mortised bench dog holes. The top is about 90 inches long, 18 inches wide up to the 6-inch-wide tool tray, 4 inches thick at the edge, and 2½ inches thick at its center. The drawer measures about 58 × 19½ × 8 inches. The workbench's height from the floor is 35½ inches, and its weight is 352 pounds.

The Ulmia Master Cabinetmaker's Bench (Illus. 4-6) is also made of red beech and features two large vises and square-mortised dog holes. The top is about 84 inches long, 18 inches wide up to the 6-inch-wide tool tray, 4 inches thick at the edge, and 2½ inches thick at the center. Its height above the floor is 35½ inches, and its weight is 310 pounds.

Illus. 4-5. The Ulmia Ultimate Workbench.

Illus. 4-6. The Ulmia Master Cabinetmaker's Workbench.

Illus. 4-7. The Ulmia Master Carver's Bench.

The Ulmia Master Carver's Bench (Illus. 4-7) is designed with a transferable tool tray and two rows of dog holes on either side of the bench. These holes interact with the two dog holes in the end vise so that a flat workpiece can be gripped with four-point contact. The bench measures about 72 inches long, 23 inches wide, 3 inches thick at its edge, and 1½ inches thick at its center. Its height above the floor is 34½ inches, and its weight is 215 pounds. (The Ulmia workbenches are available from Woodcraft Supply.)

The Black & Decker Workmate is a different kind of factory-made bench that is designed to be folded up and compactly stored between jobs. There are many different models to choose among. Illus. 4-8–4-10 show three different models which are worth considering. Workmate benches are unusual in that they are portable, modest in size, and have clamping versatility. If you have been using a plain bench with a tiny machinist's vise and have just upgraded to a Workmate bench, then being able to secure a workpiece between dogs or in the center slot will prove to be inspiring.

Illus. 4-9. The Black & Decker Workmate 85.

Illus. 4-8. The Black & Decker Workmate 350.

Illus. 4-10. The Black & Decker Workmate 2000.

Shop-Made Workbenches

The customized, shop-made bench is my favorite style of bench. These benches truly reflect the personality of the individual woodworker and the type of work done. The variety of design possibilities, materials, and construction methods is endless.

Benches can be made of many woods. For durability, stability and attractiveness, maple is my first preference. Other suitable woods are fine-grained oak, ash, birch or beech. It's not necessary to use the same wood throughout the bench. Cherry makes a good accent wood, and a maple top will sit quite nicely upon oak legs. Some woodworkers like to cover their bench's laminated maple top with tempered hardboard, a flat, smooth material that can be replaced as it wears out.

Stanley offers plans for two workbenches: the Child-Size Workbench (Illus. 4-11) and the Stanley Workbench (Illus. 4-12). Stanley's 12-page plans offer step-by-step information for building the benches.

A shop-made bench is not only aesthetically pleasing and functional, it also provides a wonderful learning experience. When you make a bench, you will have to design it for a specific purpose, make a bill of materials and cutting list, and use joinery and gluing and clamping techniques. Also, it is the perfect project on which to test your skills. It is much better to learn how to laminate by constructing a bench top than to experience this process

Illus. 4-11. Stanley Tool has plans for this child's workbench.

Illus. 4-12. Stanley Tool has plans for the Stanley Workbench.

while making a fine piece of furniture destined for your dining room.

If, for example, you choose to build a 24 × 60-inch workbench, you will have to do the following: select vises and other hardware, make a laminated top, and use joinery for the framework.

To illustrate how the choice of vise affects the design and construction of a workbench, let's assume two Record vises are being used. Generally, the large vise is bolted to the front edge and the smaller vise is bolted to the side edge of the bench top. Fitting the vise can be complicated if you don't work out a solution before beginning construction. If you hold one of the vises against a bench top, you will notice that the vise jaws will probably be either higher or lower than the thickness of the bench top, and the rear vise jaw is not flush with the bench. Both of these conditions have to be dealt with for a proper fit.

The height of the vise jaw can be controlled by installing a spacer board between the bench and vise. But, first you'll need to decide if the vise jaws will be flush or recessed to the bench surface. There are two reasons why it is preferable to recess the top of the jaws. First, since the bench top has to be occasionally reflattened and resur-

faced, there is the possibility that either the belt sander or hand plane could grind or bang into the metal jaw edge if the vise is flush to the surface. Secondly, there is the possibility that exposed metal surfaces on the bench top will be cut into with sharp chisels. On the other hand, if the vise edge is recessed then there is a gap between it and the bench surface. You can easily correct this, however, by covering the jaw surface with wood.

The best approach is to have a continuous front edge on the bench top which is not interrupted by a block of wood on a vise. To accomplish this and still cover the recess on the top edge, mount the vise to the bench and then make a front edge board that fits around the vise and becomes the front edge of the bench. This front edge board is not glued on; instead, it's attached with screws. Illus. 4-13 shows a view from under the bench. The vise is mounted to the spacer board with lag screws, and the vise jaw is enclosed in the front strip of wood. Note the number of plugged screw holes in the bench. Lumber is frequently moved across this board and it is constantly gouged with tools, so if it's attached by screws it can be occasionally replaced. The edge boards on this bench have been replaced once in the 15 years it has been used.

Illus. 4-13. An under-the-workbench view of a Record vise installation. Note that the vise jaws are covered with wood.

Designing Your Bench

Before starting to build a bench, first decide for what woodworking tasks and how the bench is to be used. Each type of woodworking has unique requirements, and the bench should be built with those requirements in mind. General woodworking, furniture making, carving, making miniatures, making musical instruments, inlay work and marquetry, lathe turning, and restoration are a few of the types of woodworking for which a bench can be built.

Many quality benches, such as the bench shown in Illus. 4-14 that was made by Jon Arno, are made of pine or fir and plywood. Jon's bench incorporates plywood storage with pine-fronted drawers and a top of solid-core plywood with a fibreboard cover. The bench height is just lower than the height of the table saw. If necessary, this allows workpieces to be supported as they come off the saw. Also, the bench is modular in design so that it can be moved or have additional storage added to it. The top is not mounted to the storage units; it is secured by its own weight.

Pete Kolettis, another woodworker, used an old desk and added a plywood platform to make a work surface on which to make his marquetry pieces (Illus. 4-15). He screwed a $\frac{1}{2} \times 10 \times 14$-inch piece of plywood to a short

Illus. 4-14. The top of this workbench rests upon modular storage units.

Illus. 4-15. This small table for making marquetry pieces is clamped to a bench top.

piece of wood to raise the working level to a comfortable height. The plywood has a V-shaped cut which ends in a ½-inch hole. The marquetry pieces are placed over the opening and sawn with a fretsaw with a fine blade. This arrangement could be clamped to any table or bench top, whether it is located in the basement or on the porch.

Dick Dermody's workshop occupies very little space in one corner of the basement. He primarily carves half-ship

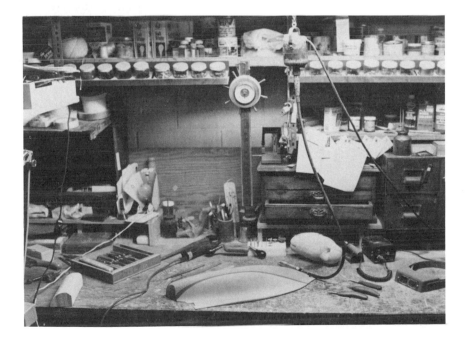

Illus. 4-16. This carver's work station provides easy access to tools and other frequently used materials.

hulls, chip carvings, and small relief carvings. His workbench is constructed of several thicknesses of plywood that rest upon a typical leg frame with storage shelf (Illus. 4-16).

Scott Gruenberg also does carving. But instead of making a traditional workbench, he made a work station with a drawer and built-in fan (Illus. 4-17). The fan is enclosed in the upper compartment (Illus. 4-18) and draws air and dust through the open slot in the front under the tray for the bits (Illus. 4-19). The dust is then drawn up into a furnace filter and exits in the rear. The fan is so powerful and dust removal so efficient that Scott is planning to install a screen in the front slot, so that small-cutting bits won't be pulled into the compartment.

Mark Nathenson created a unique work platform by attaching a wooden top to the pedestal of a dentist chair (Illus. 4-20). Raising and lowering the workpiece via foot pedals allows him to position the work area at a comfortable level.

Norm Peterson does commercial woodworking and has no need for the "traditional" bench. He does, however, need a large, flat area for sanding and routing. Since both of these activities generate volumes of dust and debris, he built a dust-collecting system into the work station (Illus. 4-21). The top is slotted so that the collector pulls debris downward, and then into the collector on the left side. The slots also serve as a place for attaching "bench stops" and other securing devices. The work station is large enough for several people to work simultaneously and still keep tools and safety equipment close at hand. While this system may not replace the traditional

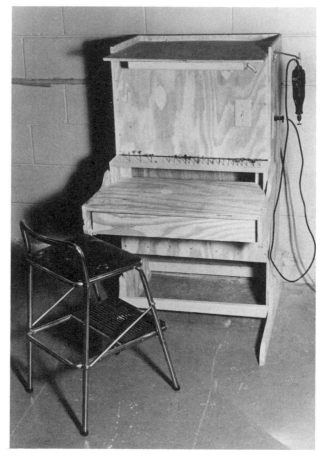

Illus. 4-17. This carver's work station has a built-in fan suction that pulls dust away from the carver. It also features a built-in light and an AC receptacle.

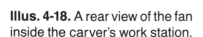

Illus. 4-18. A rear view of the fan inside the carver's work station.

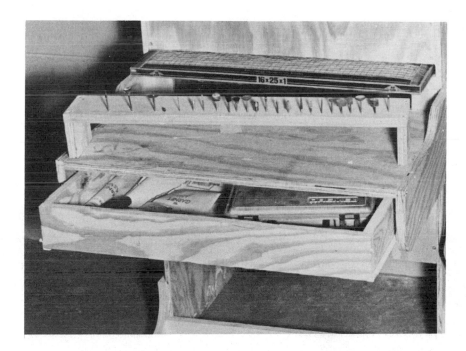

Illus. 4-19. A close-up of a work station that features a drawer, bit storage, and an air filter.

Illus. 4-20 (above left). The pedestal of a dentist's chair is used as an adjustable work surface. **Illus. 4-21 (above right).** A router work station with a built-in dust-collecting system.

bench, it does emphasize the fact that the workbench should be designed to meet the woodworkers specific needs.

Another consideration when designing your work-bench is the position of vises, drawers, dog holes and hold-downs. Workbenches are commonly thought of as tabletops with one or two vises attached to the edges. There are, however, many other methods for securing

Illus. 4-22. This antique workbench has a sliding and adjustable workpiece support.

Illus. 4-23. Twelve-inch-long pipe clamps are mounted to the front of this workbench.

workpieces or dealing with specialized work situations. For instance, some historic benches had a vertically mounted front board that slid across the bench front. This board had a row of holes drilled into it for inserting a dowel. A long workpiece could then be clamped into the front vise and be supported by the dowel (Illus. 4-22).

John Kirchner's clamping system is shown in Illus. 4-23 and 4-24. He has attached pipe fittings to the front edge of his bench for holding the threaded end of pipe clamps. This allows him to secure a harp body for planing and other detail work.

Using a vise, even one with a quick action, takes time. If designing a bench for limited production work such as edge-trimming or routing, consider a vacuum clamp sys-

tem. These units grip the workpiece by suction, don't mar the work surface, and are very fast to use (Illus. 4-25).

Determining Your Bench Measurements

When determining the bench measurements, take into consideration your height, arm length, project sizes and weights, and shop space. Some woodworkers prefer low benches regardless of any of these variables. Some woodworkers want to be able to approach the bench from and use all four sides as work areas; others want the bench positioned snug against a wall.

There are numerous charts and graphs that indicate optimal table heights for the ubiquitous "average" work conditions and the "average" size woodworker. However,

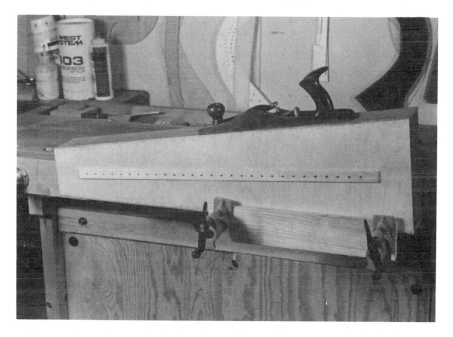

Illus. 4-24. A pipe clamp system holding a harp body for planing.

Illus. 4-25. A vacuum clamp holding a wooden arrow.

many woodworkers do not fit into these designations. Adding to this confusion are all the instructors and experts who profess to know the optimal measurements for a workbench.

There is an alternative approach for determining the measurements for your workbench. First, decide upon the bench location and whether the bench will be positioned against a wall or be freestanding. Second, consider your own body size and strength. If you are robust and can move heavy wood around, then a high and wide bench might be your preference. If you are shorter, then a lower bench might be preferable.

With those thoughts in mind, let's consider how the bench feels as you perform your specific woodworking tasks on it. Make a mock-up of a bench with sawhorses and a stack of boards, and create a bench height that you feel comfortable at. Take no height measurement at this time. Now stand a 6 to 8-inch board on it's edge and slide a bladeless plane on the board's edge. Lay the board flat and repeat the same procedure. Continue in this fashion using unplugged sanders, plate-joinery tools, drills, and anything else you think you might be using at the bench. Adjust the stack of wood on the sawhorses for the approximate height, and assess how you physically feel at various work heights. Ask yourself the following questions: How do my back and arms feel when I'm stretched out, bent over, or working erect?

As you find comfortable working heights, measure the heights for all the various tools and wood applications. If you find that there is a wide range of heights, you may want to go through the entire procedure once again to check which height is the most comfortable overall. And if the measurements are similar, average them and use this as the height for your workbench.

Although there is never one perfect height for all applications, selecting the one which feels most comfortable for the most common applications is the best compromise. I did meet one woodworker, however, who felt that there were two best working heights, and his solution for having both was rather clever. His workbench was constructed so that its height was slightly less than the average height. Then, he placed a railroad tie beam on the floor in front of the bench, much like a bar rail. When planing long boards, he used the beam as a higher floor to walk upon.

Once you have determined your ideal bench height, it's time to determine the bench width. This is simpler because it can be primarily based upon the type of work to be done. If you plan to build chairs, make the bench wider than the widest part of a chair. If you plan to use the bench as a gluing platform for inlay surfaces or drawer constructions, then use the dimensions of these surfaces to determine the bench width.

Other variables worth noting when pondering bench width are how and where the leg construction will attach to the underside of the bench top. I use quick-action clamps to secure workpieces to the front, back, and sides of my bench. In order to have a clamping surface underneath the bench top, I designed my bench so that the top overhangs the leg framework about 4 inches.

Illus. 4-26. The disassembled vise and screw mechanism on a vise integrated into a workbench.

Bench Vises

Before finalizing the design for your bench top, take another moment to look at the variety of vises and other accessory pieces such as edge clamps, bench stops, and hold downs that can be attached to the bench.

General-purpose and joinery benches used for furniture construction usually have a front and side vise. Bench vises are available in two basic styles. One style is integrated into the workbench, and the other style is bolted onto the workbench. The integrated style usually consists of a metal housing and screw mechanism (Illus. 4-26), and the bench top must be designed specifically to accommodate the vise. For those who would like to build their bench with this type of vise, Woodcraft Supply sells bench hardware and vise plans. Illus. 4-27 and 4-28 show examples of this type of vise installed at the end of a workbench.

The type of vise which is designed to be bolted directly to the bench requires no special construction plans. These vises are very popular, and a large variety is avail-

Illus. 4-27. An assembled and mounted vise.

Illus. 4-28. A custom-made vise with two rows of bench-dog holes.

able. Excellent choices are the Record rapid action vises, Jorgensen Rapid Acting bench vises, and the Veritas Tucker vise.

The Record and Jorgensen vises are very good products because of several features. They are both well made and both have a mechanism which allows you to quickly open or close them without having to turn the vise handle. Simply squeeze the engaging lever, pull open the vise, insert the workpiece, slide the vise closed, and then turn the handle to completely secure the workpiece.

John Danielson's workbench is a beautiful example of a shop-made workbench (Illus. 4-29). It is made of maple

Illus. 4-29. This large workbench has an antique Emmert Patternmaker's vise.

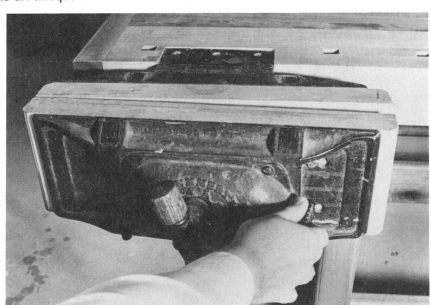

Illus. 4-30. The jaws on the Emmert vise can be adjusted to different angles.

and oak and features a classic end vise and an Emmert Patternmaker's vise. The Emmert Patternmaker's vise was first introduced around the end of the last century, and has many innovative features which allow the workpiece to be secured in numerous orientations. The vise can be rotated or tilted and the jaws can be angled. There are four dogs on the top of the vise for securing workpieces, and there is a smaller set of jaws on the bottom of the vise. There is even an angled jaw piece for fitting within the standard jaws. This is an extraordinary vise that is very helpful. The Emmert vise is occasionally found in antique tool sources and is prized by collectors (Illus. 4-30–4-35).

Illus. 4-31. The Emmert vise partially rotated.

Illus. 4-32. The Emmert vise partially tilted.

Illus. 4-33. The Emmert vise reversed to access a pair of small vise jaws.

Illus. 4-34. The Emmert vise in normal position with four raised dog posts securing a workpiece.

Illus. 4-35. The Emmert vise with its jaws in a horizontal position.

The Veritas Tucker vise, a contemporary version of the Emmert vise, is more sleekly styled and is made of mod ern materials. It, too, offers several features which are not found on the typical vise. The Tucker vise can rotate 360 degrees as well as tilt from vertical to horizontal. Its front jaws pivot to hold tapered workpieces, and the jaws each have two built-in dogs. Jaw sizes of 13, 5½, and 2¾ inches are available (Illus. 4-37–4-41).

If the workbench is to be used for carving, it needs to be designed to accommodate ways of holding a carving piece. Power arms, carver's screws and universal vises are some of the options available. The universal vise shown in Illus. 4-42 has bolts on either side of its jaws that can be loosened with a wrench so that they can be adjusted to hold angled pieces such as a tapered leg. The universal vise raises the workpiece approximately 10 inches above the bench top, so bench height is very critical for using this vise. Otherwise, the workpiece may be held too high in the air for comfortable work. The universal vise is secured to the bench by a threaded rod through a bench dog hole and a large wing nut.

Also consider the overall size of the carving piece. If you plan to carve long, narrow pieces, then a universal vise or carving vise might be adequate. However, if you plan to carve three-dimensional pieces, carver's screws or power arms might be more appropriate.

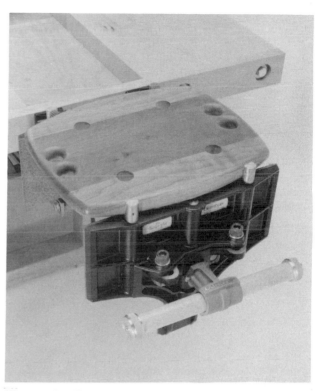

Illus. 4-37. The workpiece is secured between the four vise dogs.

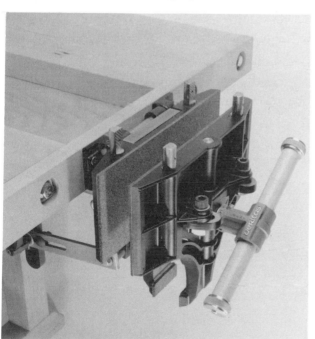

Illus. 4-36. A modern Tucker vise from Veritas Tools. Note the four dogs and the lower small jaws.

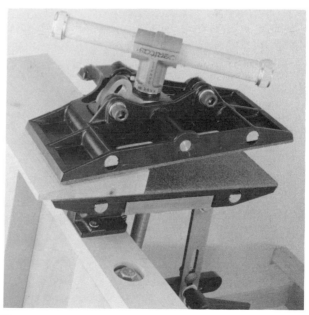

Illus. 4-38. The Tucker vise in a rotated position and securing an angled workpiece.

Illus. 4-39 (left). The Tucker vise holding a workpiece at an angle. **Illus. 4-40 (above).** The vise's small jaws are in their vertical position.

Illus. 4-41. The vise's jaws are in their horizontal position.

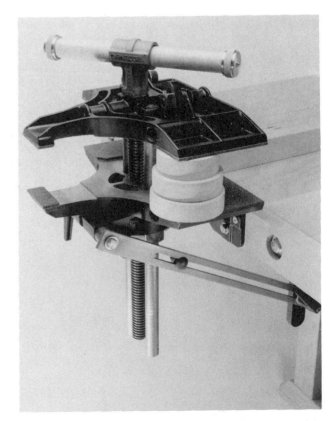

Illus. 4-42. This universal vise is secured through workbench dog holes. Its jaws are adjustable for different angles.

Making a Bench Top

The laminations on a bench top must be flat and square. In addition, pay attention to the following construction guidelines: First, cut each lamination to some measurable thickness so that it can be later used as a visual aid when the bench is used. Laminations that are either ½, ¾, or 1 inch can be used to determine the rough measurements of a board or workpiece. For example, place a drawer on a bench with 1-inch-thick laminations and simply count the number of laminations to determine the drawer's rough measurement. Second, when setting out the individual lamination boards, lay them out so that their grain patterns are running in the same direction. Randomly oriented grain will result in some boards having a rough surface due to torn grain and other boards being smooth after the bench top is either machine- or hand-planed.

Be very careful when gluing up the laminations for a bench top. Use a square to check that all edges are square. Use a caliper to be certain that the individual boards are the same thickness from end to end, and the surfaces are parallel to each other. Boards that are not parallel will glue up into a curved shape.

Considerable clamp force is required to properly glue up a wide lamination. To make it easier when gluing and to keep the laminations tightly fitted together, drill holes though each of the lamination boards so that threaded rods can be used. Before any drilling is done, plan the location of vises and dog holes so that there will be no interference between holes, screws, or other hardware. Make the holes' diameters larger than the rod diameter. For example, if using a ⅜-inch rod, drill ⅝- or ¾-inch-diameter holes. The oversized hole will allow some positioning adjustments of the lamination boards during glue-up. Countersink the holes in the two outside lamination boards. The two end boards can be covered with single lamination boards after the main part of the bench top is glued up. Have enough pipe or bar clamps so that they can be placed every 4 or 5 inches along the length of the laminations.

Make the first laminations as perfect as possible. This is because since the first lamination is glued first, it cannot be readjusted much when the last lamination is glued. It's very difficult to hammer those first laminations into a new position once the glue sets.

The following is an effective glue-up procedure. After drilling the laminations for the threading rods, make plate joiner holes every 12 to 14 inches along the upper edge of the laminations. The biscuit plates are useful for alignment purposes, and they will help keep the top surface reasonably flat. Next, thoroughly clean all the lamination boards. Be certain that the plate and rod holes are chip- and dust-free. Set out the laminations in the order of their position, and draw pencil lines over the locations of the rod holes. These lines are used as reference lines when gluing up.

On a flat surface, set out clamps about 12 inches apart. Use a slow-setting glue (for example, a white carpenter's

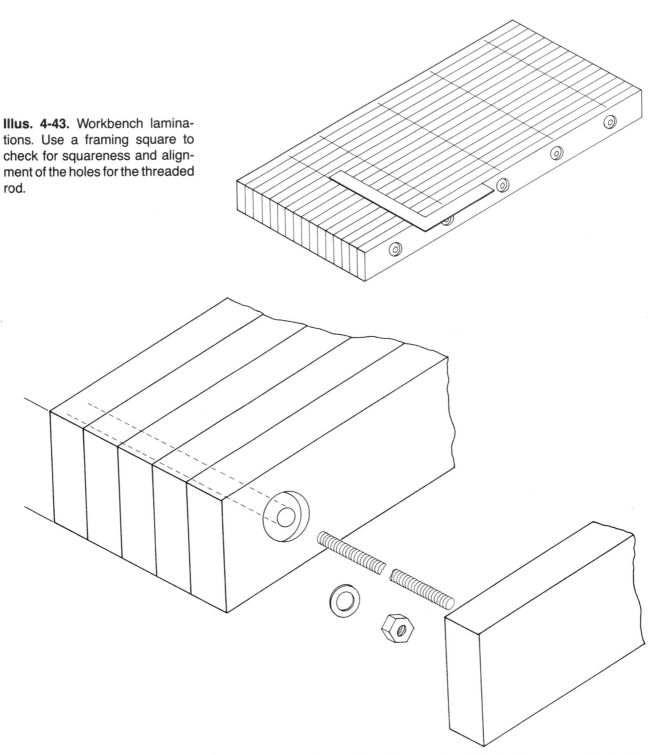

Illus. 4-43. Workbench laminations. Use a framing square to check for squareness and alignment of the holes for the threaded rod.

Illus. 4-44. A close-up of the workbench corner, featuring laminations with holes for threaded rod and exposed laminations that have a countersunk hole for a washer and nut. Cap board is glued onto laminations after the threaded rods are all in place. The other side of the workbench has identical features.

glue). Spread a liberal coat of glue on the first lamination and prepare to work quickly. Glue both sides of the next board, and place it and the biscuit plates against the previous board.

After placing several laminations, use a rafter square and check that the reference lines are straight. Continue on until all laminations are in place. Lightly tighten the clamps and insert the threaded rods. The glue may make it difficult to push the rods through, so place a nut and washer on one end and hammer the rod through. Put a nut and washer on the other end, and tighten the rods in place. Once this is done, place a top row of clamps in place and tighten. Finally, retighten the threaded rods and clamps.

When the glue becomes rubbery, remove the clamps and scrape off the excess glue. Remove as much glue as possible. Replace the clamps and allow sufficient time for the glue to dry before doing any further work. It's best to remove the squeezed-out glue at this time, simply because it becomes more difficult the longer the glue dries. Hardened glue on any surface, and especially on a lamination, is difficult to remove. Glue collects on recessed laminations, between higher edges, and is extremely difficult to remove. Belt-sanding will only cause the glue to heat up and ooze. And, if you want to take the bench top to a mill shop for sanding and flattening, they will expect you to have removed the excess glue so that it will not ruin their expensive wide belts. (Otherwise, they will probably expect you to pay for the belts.)

Many different approaches can be taken in making a workbench top. The following are two examples. In the first, a woodworker decided to use a No. 8 jointer's plane and No. 6 fore plane to hand-plane both the top and the underside of the workbench top to perfect flatness. The bench top was placed on sturdy sawhorses to prevent it from bouncing as it was being worked on. The bottom surface was planed first. It provided a good practice area, and would later be used as a reference point for making the top surface parallel.

The first planing action was done diagonally across the surface, working from the center to the edges. The entire surface had a chevron pattern on it, after the first rough planing. As the plane work continued, the planing action became more parallel to the direction of the grain. Once the bottom surface was finished, the bench top was flipped over. The top surface was prepared in a similar manner with the exception that the surface was planed down to a measured pencil line that was indexed from the lower surface.

In the second example, another woodworker decided to hand-plane the top surface flat and then take the bench top to a mill shop to have the underside drum-sanded. In this situation, the top surface (not the bottom surface) was prepared because as a drum sander ends its pass at the end of a board, it sometimes comes down over the edge of the board and rounds the edge over.

The frame of the workbench has to be strong so that the bench can withstand surface blows and the lateral stress, or racking, which results from plane and chisel action. The lateral motion of planing a board can quite possibly cause the bench to "quiver" more than any other activity at the bench, even on a 300-pound bench.

Proper joinery is required to solidify the bench. Most bench frames are built with mortise-and-tenon joints, and the stretchers between are further reinforced with bolts that go through the mortise and tenons.

When I built my bench, the frame consisted of legs, feet, and stretchers. However, there was a slight side-to-side racking when I planed workpieces. To eliminate this motion, I disassembled the frame and added two additional pieces: a stretcher piece between the two rear legs, just under the bench top, and a piece of ½-inch plywood, as shown in Illus. 4-45. I routed a ⅜-inch-deep groove into the two rear stretchers and legs, inserted the plywood into this space, and reassembled the bench. Adding the plywood stopped all racking. The bench definitely works better now.

Shop Space and the Workbench

Shop space often determines the size, number, and types of workbenches used in the shop. In larger shops, it's not uncommon to have a low bench, perhaps 8 × 4 × 2 feet, that is used for assembly work or vacuum clamping. There might even be a special table or framework for gluing purposes, as shown in Illus. 4-46. If you don't have the space for several special-purpose benches and plan to use your bench for many purposes, be certain to factor these requirements into the shape of the bench.

My bench is the flattest surface in my shop, and I use it for gluing everything from drawers and tabletops to chairs (Illus. 4-47). Since I like to use Jorgensen steel I bar clamps because of their strength, rigidity, and self-standing design for gluing work, I designed my bench top so that part of it can accommodate 18-inch bar clamps and another part can accommodate 24-inch bar clamps. Because I frequently use my bench as a gluing surface, I store my bar clamps near the bench so that they are always accessible when I'm working.

The bench can also be used for a variety of other clamping applications. As shown in Illus. 4-48, on the

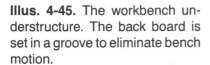

Illus. 4-45. The workbench understructure. The back board is set in a groove to eliminate bench motion.

Illus. 4-46. A clamping rack designed to hold numerous bar clamps.

Illus. 4-47. The bar clamps rest upon the workbench.

Illus. 4-48. Various clamping operations demonstrated upon the workbench.

right end of the bench, three pieces cut with a scroll saw are held down by a clamped strip of wood. This technique also works for gluing applications where the object is at the center of the bench and the throat size of the standard clamp isn't deep enough to reach.

Another gluing technique, which is shown in the background in Illus. 4-48, consists of securing stacks of boards between the bench and "quick-action" clamps. Also, at the center of the bench two quick-action clamps are used to secure a dovetailed drawer. The drawer is resting upon the flat bench top to ensure a proper shape. At the left side of the bench in Illus. 4-48 a four-board tabletop is being glued together. Two bar clamps are under the workpiece and face towards the room. Another clamp is on top and faces the wall. Changing clamp orientation is a common method for ensuring that clamping pressure is more uniform in nature. Also note the strips of wood between the workpiece and the clamps; these wood strips help to protect the edges of the work-piece and distribute the clamping pressure more evenly along the edge of the workpiece. A triangle and numbers are marked on the surface of the workpiece in chalk to ensure proper positioning.

There are two additional factors that must be considered when gluing together projects. First, if glue "bleeds" and comes in contact with iron clamps, the wood will be stained. Always place a strip of waxed paper between clamps and the workpiece to prevent any staining. Second, when placing a bar clamp over the top surface, use biscuit plates as spacers to keep the clamp away from the glue. Biscuit plates are thin and of a consistent thickness, so they won't interfere with gluing.

When looking at the photographs of my bench, you may have noticed that the front vise of my bench is on the right side and the end vise is on the left side. Most other photos and illustrations show just the opposite orientation. They are oriented on my bench as such because I'm left-handed.

CHAPTER FIVE
Power Tools

Since the variety of power tools that is available to the hobbyist and professional is enormous, it helps to simplify the selection process by categorizing power tools into two groups: processing tools and finishing tools. Processing tools are those which allow you to cut or shape raw material and break it down into manageable pieces. The list includes table saws, radial arm saws, circular saws, band saws, and jointer/planers. Finishing tools are tools which refine wood into the final workpiece. This list includes routers, router tables, lathes, stationary drills, hand drills, plate joiners, joinery machines, joinery jigs, shapers, sanders, scroll saws, and power carving tools. Many of the processing tools, such as the radial arm saw,

table saw, band saw, and jointer/planer, can also be used as finishing tools if they are accurately adjusted and used for precise cuts. The following tool review is not meant to be comprehensive in scope or variety. Instead, it is a review of the principal tools and machines found in small, general-purpose shops.

Table Saws

The table saw can be the single most used machine in a workshop (Illus. 5-1). It can be used to cut sheets of plywood, shorten long boards, resaw certain thicknesses

Illus. 5-1. A Delta 10-inch tilting-arbor Unisaw.

of wood, make fancy joinery, and for many other tasks. The table saw can be set up to make repetitive cuts, and used to make an unlimited number of the same workpiece. It is possible to replace the saw blade with dado cutters, and some table saws can be used with moulding head cutters.

Table saws are available in a range of sizes. The size of the table saw is determined by the size of the table saw blade. Generally, an 8- or 10-inch blade is considered standard, but table saws are also available in 12-, 14-, and 16-inch sizes. Some table saws are referred to as "contractor" saws (Illus. 5-2). These saws are smaller and lighter than a cabinetmaker's saw. This allows the saw to be easily lifted in and out of a truck or van for transport to and from a job site. The contractor saw is not just for tradesmen; in fact, it is more than adequate for most home shops.

One-to-two horsepower motors are satisfactory for

Illus. 5-2. A Sears 10-inch contractor's saw.

Illus. 5-3. A Biesemeyer fence.

most table saw work. Generally, motors greater than two horsepower are wired for 220 volts. The on/off switches should be in a convenient and safe location. Some switches have an oversized off button, so that the button can be easily found in emergencies.

There are certain features you should look for when shopping for a table saw. The table surface should be flat. A table that is not flat will cause odd-angled cuts and produce workpieces that will not fit together correctly. Table saws should have guards which are unobtrusive and do not inhibit the view of the blade. The fence should be ruggedly made, easy to use, parallel to the saw blade, and simple to adjust (Illus. 5-3). The better fences are secured to both the front and rear table rails. The fence should also sit flush to the table surface. If there is a gap, thin workpieces will slide under the fence and be poorly cut.

The mitre gauge bar should fit neatly within the table groove, and should have little or no looseness. It should also be of sufficient length and able to support both small and large workpieces (Illus. 5-4). A mitre gauge with a drop stop will allow you to make accurate, repetitive cuts. And the process of calibrating the mitre angles should be simple, so that a specific angle can be set and accurately reset.

Other features which enhance the use of the table saw are adequate table size, a sliding table, moulding heads, and dust-collection ports. Many table saws are fitted with additional tables that are usually to the side and rear of the saw. This results in a larger work area for moving and cutting sheet materials. The Powermatic saw shown in Illus. 5-5 has been fitted with a Biesemeyer fence, guard, and extension rail system which includes a longer support arm for the guard.

Radial Arm Saws

The radial arm saw is often mistakenly considered a cutoff saw, a saw used only for house framing, or as a substitute for the table saw. While the radial arm saw can be used for all these purposes, it is more versatile. Its uses include cutting long boards to shorter lengths, rip cuts, and moulding and sanding applications.

Many radial arm saws are used only for cutoff work because their owner's failed to make several critical adjustments to ensure that the saw would perform accurately. The radial arm saw is designed such that a motor is suspended from the movable arm so that the blade can be oriented perpendicular to the table (for both straight and angled cuts), horizontal to the table, and parallel to the table stop. Because of the movement necessary for different orientations of both the motor and blade, certain alignment adjustments must be performed. If these adjustments are performed regularly, the radial arm saw will cut straight. If not performed, then the radial arm saw is

Illus. 5-4. An Accu-Miter gauge from J.D.S. Co.

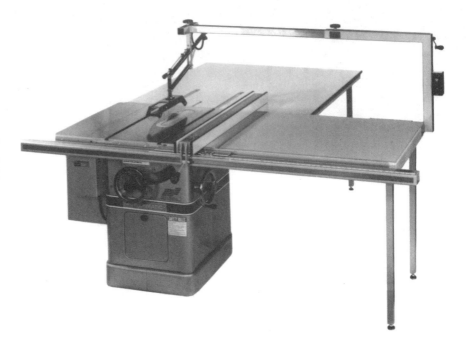

Illus. 5-5. This Powermatic saw has been fitted with a Biesemeyer fence, rail and guard system.

Illus. 5-6. A Sears 10-inch radial arm saw.

only useful for cutting boards to rough lengths.

There are several features you should look for when shopping for a radial arm saw. The stand, which is typically an open-structured design, should be rigid and stable. The controls should be convenient, and the adjustment screws should be accessible and easy to adjust. The positional stops (90 degrees, 45 degrees, etc.) should be indexed and adjustable. The motor should have a brake for quick blade stoppage, and the guards should work simply and not hinder the view of the cutting operation.

Ten- and 12-inch saw blades are generally preferable for the smaller shop, although radial arm saws are available in larger 14-, 16- and 18-inch blade sizes. Recently, smaller tabletop radial arm saws, such as the 8½-inch saw shown in Illus. 5-7, have become popular for smaller shops. Radial arm saws usually have 2-to-3-horsepower, single-phase motors, although larger-capacity saws are available with 7½-horsepower, three-phase motors.

Since the radial arm saw is useful for cutting long boards, it is beneficial to have extension tables on either side of the saw. These not only support the longer boards, but the area beneath can be used for storage (Illus. 5-8).

Common accessories for the radial arm saw include moulding head and cutters, sanding discs and drums, extension tables, dado heads, and workpiece stops. A positional stop along the back stop is shown in Illus. 5-8.

Illus. 5-7. A Sears bench-top 8¼-inch radial arm saw.

Illus. 5-8. This radial arm saw has a long work table area, storage space, and Biesemeyer stops.

Circular Saws

The circular saw is an inexpensive tool useful for cutting longer boards into shorter lengths or for cutting sheet materials. However, it is not recommended as a substitute for either the table saw or radial arm saw. The circular saw is frequently used in the construction business, and most tradesmen prefer quality saws that are powerful and rugged (Illus. 5-9 and 5-10). These hand-held saws are available in a range of motor and blade sizes. However, standard-size saws have 1½ to 3 horse-powers and 7¼- or 8¼-inch-diameter blades.

Mitre Saws

The mitre and compound mitre saws are bench-top tools that offer a greater degree of accuracy than the circular saw provides. These saws are primarily used for cutting trim and moulding; however, they can also be used to cut narrow lumber to shorter lengths. The mitre saw (Illus. 5-11) is used with the workpiece positioned on the table against the fence, and often the workpiece is clamped in place. The saw can also be rotated to either side to make angled cuts.

Illus. 5-9. A Sears Sawmill 7¼-inch, 2¾-horsepower circular saw.

Illus. 5-10. A Skilsaw 8¼-inch worm-drive saw with a 60-degree bevelling angle.

Illus. 5-11. A Skilsaw 10-inch mitre saw.

The compound mitre saw (Illus. 5-12 and 5-13) is similar to the mitre saw except that the saw blade can also be tilted for bevel cuts. The Hitachi compound mitre saw is positioned on the end of two rails which slide back and forth for greater cutting capacity.

When used in commercial applications, the mitre and compound mitre saws are permanently set up for specific cuts. Shops that make window parts, floor trim, or picture frames have long tables to support the workpieces and use extension rails and end stops to achieve accurate, repetitive cuts (Illus. 5-14).

Band Saws

The band saw is another versatile tool that is useful for cutting a variety of materials (Illus. 5-15). Depending upon blade type and speed, band saws can be used to cut wood and man-made wood material, plastics, fibreboard, cardboard, and soft metals. Depending upon the size and tooth pattern of the blade, the band saw can be used to make straight or curved cuts in a range of wood thicknesses.

Cabinetmakers commonly use the band saw to rip long workpieces, resaw a board into thinner sections, and cut curves and odd-shaped pieces. The band saw is even used to cut tenons and other similar joints. Lathe turners use the band saw to shape turning pieces into their prelimi-

nary round shape, or, if turning spindles, to take the long edges off a workpiece. Carvers use the band saw to remove excess wood and to shape the preliminary form before carving is started.

Illus. 5-12. A Sears 10-inch, 2-horsepower compound mitre saw.

Illus. 5-13. A Hitachi sliding 8½-inch, 1.5-horsepower compound mitre saw.

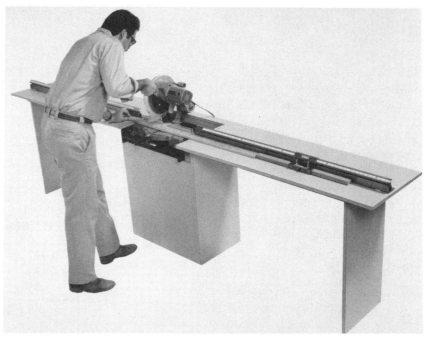

Illus. 5-14. This mitre saw is mounted to a long table. Note that Myte-R-Kut extension fences and positional side gauging stops are being used.

Band saws are available in a range of sizes. The size of the band saw is determined by the horizontal distance between the blade and frame. The height between the table and the upper housing is typically from 5 to 10 inches. Most band saws have two wheels, one above and one below the table, and ¾ to 1½ horsepower motors. Band saws need less-powerful motors than either the table saw or the radial arm saw because there is less blade cutting the wood. One exception is when wide boards are

being resawn and the blade is cutting wood 4 to 8 inches thick at one time. If a low-horsepower band saw is used, it will cut more slowly.

A small, bench-top band saw is available for shops that make small items or have limited work area. These band saws do not require a large motor because their cutting capacities are less than the larger saws. The saw shown in Illus. 5-16 can cut wood up to 3 inches thick and 10 inches wide.

Illus. 5-16. A Sears bench-top 10-inch band saw with a ⅓-horsepower motor.

The general-purpose shop should have at least two different blades for the band saw: a ¼- and a ½-inch-wide blade, each with a skip-tooth pattern. The ¼-inch blade is useful for making a variety of curved cuts. The ½-inch blade is most efficient for rip cuts and resawing. Depending upon the band-saw model, blades are available in widths from ¹⁄₁₆ to 1 inch.

Few accessories are available for most band saws. The most popular are circle-cutting guides, mitre guides, and spacer (or height-increasing) attachments.

When shopping for a band saw, consider the following: Can the blades be changed easily? Does the blade guide slide smoothly? Are the blade guides roller bearings or steel blocks? Is there a dust-collection port?

Jointers/Planers

The jointer and planer are listed here together because they are extremely useful when used together. One surface of a board can be prepared on the jointer before the board is fed through the planer. This procedure allows you to flatten one side of the board and produce a flat reference side before planing. When the flat reference side of the board is fed through the planer with the rough side exposed to the cutterhead, the board will come through flat, dimensioned, and parallel.

The jointer/planer is available as either two separate

Illus. 5-15. A Delta 14-inch band saw with a ¾-horsepower motor.

Illus. 5-17 (above left). A Delta 12-inch portable planer with a 15-amp motor and 2-knife cutterhead. **Illus. 5-18 (above right).** A Delta 13-inch planer with a 2-horsepower motor and 3-knife cutterhead.

Illus. 5-19. A Sears contractor 6⅛-inch jointer with a 2-horsepower motor and 3-knife cutterhead.

Illus. 5-20. A Delta 6-inch jointer with a ¾-horsepower motor and a 3-knife cutterhead.

machines or a combination machine (see Chapter 6). Planers are available in cutterhead widths of 10 to 24 inches (Illus. 5-17 and 5-18). Jointers are generally available in cutterhead widths of 4 to 16½ inches (Illus. 5-19 and 5-20). In a combination machine, the jointer and planer share the same cutterhead, which generally has a width of 10 to 16 inches.

Jointer/planers typically have a 2-to-5-horsepower, 220-volt motor. Most of these machines typically weigh from 50 pounds for the lightest to 1,500 pounds for the heaviest.

Consider the following features when looking for a jointer/planer: the overall length of the jointer beds, ease in removing and replacing cutterhead knives (some models have self-aligning and/or disposable knives), the length of the jointer fence, the feed rate of the planer, and accessories such as mortising tables and dust-collector attachments.

Routers

Routers are very popular general-purpose power tools. They can be likened to high-speed motors that come with handles. The router without specific jigs, accessories and cutters is not very effective. An almost endless variety of cutter bits and accessories is available for doing just about any woodworking function. The router is so versatile that it is almost impossible to list all of its functions. It can shape edges and cut slots, mortises, tenons, grooves, dadoes, dovetails, and box joints. It can trim plastic laminates, shape straight or curved edges, cut holes for biscuit plates, and make decorative patterns on spindle and bowl turnings.

There are many different types and sizes of routers (Illus. 5-21–5-23). There are fixed-based and plunging routers. Routers are available with collets ¼, ⅜, or ½ inch

Illus. 5-21. A Porter Cable 1½-horsepower, 23,000 rpm router. It can be used with ¼-, ⅜-, and ½-inch collet capacities.

Illus. 5-22. A Porter Cable 1½-horsepower, 23,000 rpm plunge router. It can be used with ¼-, ⅜-, and ½-inch collet capacities.

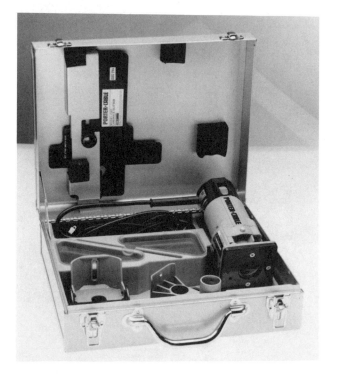

Illus. 5-23. A Porter Cable laminate trim router kit. It runs at 5.6 amp, and 30,000 rpm, and has a ¼-inch-collet capacity laminate trimmer, an off-set base, a tilt trimming base, a laminate slitter subbase and other setup pieces.

in diameter, and in horsepowers ranging from ¾ to 5. They can be variable or single speed, and small or large (Illus. 5-21–5-23.) One router is probably not enough for the small shop. A fixed-based router and a plunge router are useful for different tasks. A good choice for a small fixed-based router is one with a 1½-horsepower motor, a ¼-inch collet, several guide bushings, and an edging fence. A good choice for the larger, more powerful plunge router is one with a "soft" starting variable-speed, 3-horsepower motor, and a ½-inch collet. With these two routers, and several joinery jigs, most router applications are possible.

Router Tables

Router tables perform similarly to the hand-held router. The only difference is that the table, and not a hand, stabilizes the router. When you use a router table, you mount the router upside-down and move the work-piece into the cutter bit. In contrast, the hand-held router is held upright and the router is moved into the piece to be cut. The workpiece can be cut using the fence as a guide, a cutter bit with a ball-bearing guide, a mitre guide, or some other accessory. When you are making straight cuts with a hand-held router, you have to clamp an edge guide or a straightedge to the workpiece. Router tables make this procedure unnecessary, because the work is pushed against the table fence.

There are a variety of commercially made router tables. The Sears router table shown in Illus. 5-24 has a 14 × 24-inch work surface, fence, and sawdust collection. Illus. 5-25 shows a small Elu router and stand with a fence and a hold-down system that secures the wood from the side and the top. Both of these router tables must be secured to a workbench.

Many woodworkers make their own router tables, and the typical shop-made router table is built for a particular purpose. For example, if you will be making panels for frame-and-panel cabinet doors, the router table should have plenty of surface area to support the panel and the table's hole should be large enough to accommodate large-diameter (2- to 4-inch) cutter bits. If the same router table were used to cut ⅛-inch-wide grooves in jewelry boxes, the box could tilt into the large cutter hole and be destroyed by the cutter.

Illus. 5-26 shows a 30-inch square of medium-density fibreboard with an Incra Pro jig fence and right-angle accessory. The same router table is shown in Illus. 5-27 with the router removed to expose the center opening with the rabbeted edge. The clear base on the Hitachi

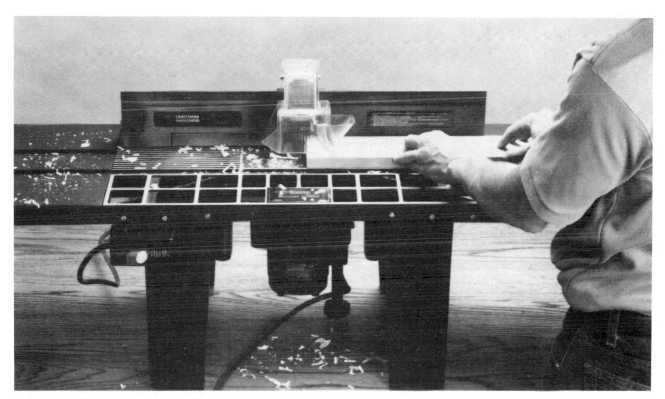

Illus. 5-24. This Sears router table is designed to accommodate a plunge router.

Illus. 5-25. This Elu 1-horsepower plunge router runs at variable speeds of 8,000 to 24,000 rpm and uses a ¼-inch collet. It is being used with a Elu spindle moulder table and a hold-down guard assembly. To use this table, you must secure it to a work surface.

Illus. 5-26 (above left). A 30 × 30-inch router tabletop with Incra Pro jig and right-angle fixture. **Illus. 5-27 (above right).** The components of a router table and a Hitachi router with a plastic sub-base which sits in a rabbeted table hole.

Illus. 5-28. A router table made from an Inca shaper tabletop. Note the long rails, the fence which fastens to both rails, and the mitre gauge.

router was shop-made of Lexan. Lexan is preferable to other plastics because it is an extremely tough and wear-resistant material that does not melt when cut or sanded (like other plastics). Lexan can be purchased at plastic supply stores or glass and window stores. Since router bases require so little material, a piece of this size is very inexpensive and can often be found in the store's scrap box. The hole was cut with a scroll saw, and the edges were shaped on a stationary belt sander.

The router table shown in Illus. 5-28 was made using

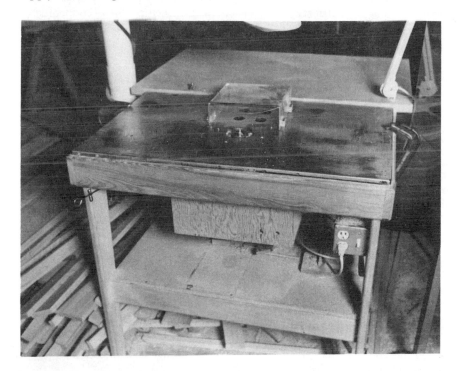

Illus. 5-29. This router table has a metal top, a plastic guard/dust collector fitting, and a router enclosed in a box.

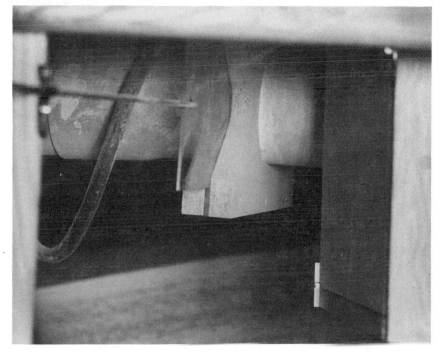

Illus. 5-30. A close-up of the custom-made dust-collector blast gate and the wire handle for opening/closing the gate.

an Inca shaper tabletop. A fence can be attached to both table rails, and the rails can be moved to either side of the table. There is an extension table mounted to the left side, and provision has been made for a mitre gauge. Most router tables are built without slots for a mitre gauge; however, the mitre gauge makes many cuts easier and safer. Ironically, the router table has taken on many aspects of the shaper, yet the one shaper feature which is often ignored is the mitre gauge.

The router table shown in Illus. 5-29 has several unique features. The tabletop is metal, with four dust-collection holes under the plastic safety-guard/dust-collection box. The plastic guard can be easily moved. Small cabinet magnets mounted to the side of the guard allow it to be held to the tabletop magnetically. The router is enclosed in a latched box which can be opened to change bits. There are two small ventilation holes in the lower right front of the box. Illus. 5-30 shows the dust-collection blast gate connected to the router box. The wire mounted to the left side of the router table opens and closes the gate.

Joinery Jigs and Machines

Joinery jigs and fixtures are a very large assemblage of both large and small, mostly single-function, devices that can be used to make joinery. Some examples are the Multi-Router (Illus. 5-31), the Leigh dovetail jig (Illus. 5-32), the Leigh multiple mortise and tenon jig (Illus. 5-33), the Keller dovetail template (Illus. 5-34), and the Record dowelling jig and Dowl-it (Illus. 5-35). These jigs and machines are used to cut dovetails, mortise and tenons, finger or box joints, splines, mitres and bevels and to drill dowel holes. Refer to magazine review articles and obtain literature from the manufacturers to discover how each jig works and what it is capable of doing. Some companies have videos showing how their products actually work.

Illus. 5-31. The Multi-Router joinery machine.

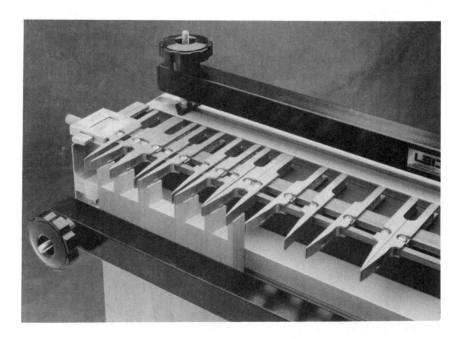

Illus. 5-32. A close-up of the Leigh dovetail jig finger assembly. The fingers are adjustable for different sizes, locations, and numbers of dovetails. One side of the finger assembly is for cutting dovetail pins, the other side is for cutting dovetail tails. The jig and a router can be used for making through, half-blind, sliding, and other styles of dovetails.

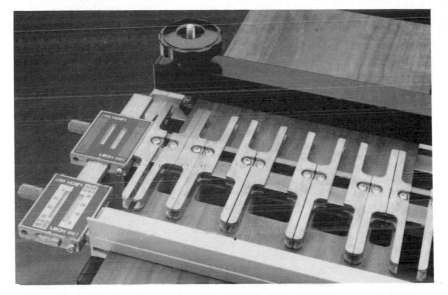

Illus. 5-33. A close-up of the Leigh multiple mortise and tenon jig. This jig requires that a plunge router be used for cutting the mortise holes.

Illus. 5-34. The Keller dovetail system. This system consists of two fixed spacing templates and two router cutters. Several other sizes of templates are available. The Keller system is principally used to cut through dovetails.

Illus. 5-35. The Dowl-It dowelling jig is clamped onto the board edge for drilling centered dowel holes. The Record dowelling jig is used for both surface and edge drilling. A stop collar is attached to the drill bit to control the depth of the hole.

Shapers

The shaper is a more sophisticated version of the router table (Illus. 5-36). In fact, in many workshops the router table is used as if it were a shaper partly because there are many large router cutters that are designed specifically for router tables. With that in mind, the principal features of routers and shapers should be compared. Routers have ¼- to ½-inch collets and turn at speeds between 10,000 to 25,000 rpm. Shapers have ½- to 1¼-inch spindles and turn at speeds between 3,000 to 10,000 rpm. Large-diameter router cutters (1½ to over 3 inches) have only ½-inch-diameter shafts. There is the danger that a large cutter will develop extremely fast speeds at its cutting edge. In fact, a 3-inch-diameter cutter on a router turning at 24,000 rpm develops speed in excess of 220 mph. By comparison, a shaper cutter turning at 6,000 rpm develops a speed of 53 mph. Routers with variable speeds can be slowed down, but they are still turning at greater rpm than the fastest turning shaper. As a rule, the shaper is the best choice for use with a large-diameter cutter. This is because its spindles are larger than the router's shafts, thus enhancing cutter stability. Also, its slower speeds make cutting safer and more controllable.

Features which enhance the use of the shaper include reversing switches, adjustable fences, concentric table inserts, hold-downs and safety guards. Many different cutters for a variety of purposes are available in both tungsten carbide and steel. The more commonly used shaper cutters are used to cut sets of frame-and-panel profiles, glue joints, door edge details, beads, coves, tongue and grooves, lock mitres, and straight and sash profiles. Those woodworkers who need a custom shape on a cutter often have a steel blank shaped into the required profile.

Lathes

One of the few woodworking endeavors done almost entirely on one machine is lathe turning. Lathe work is divided into two principal types: spindle- and bowl-turning. Spindle-turning is done between the centers of the head and tail stocks (Illus. 5-37 and 5-38). Bowls are turned primarily on the head stock. The most sought-after lathes for bowl turning have a greater vertical distance between the center of the head stock and the lathe bed. This is because large bowls are popular; and the greater the space between head stock and bed, the larger the diameter of bowl which can be turned.

Some lathes allow bowls to be mounted in an out-board location, that is, on the opposite side of the head stock. (An auxiliary tool rest must be used if larger bowls are turned in the out-board location.) Popular features on lathes are a variable-speed motor, with an emphasis on slow speeds, and a variety of tool rests and chucks. Dust-collecting fixtures, an assortment of chisels and gouges, a gooseneck lamp, and portable sanding devices are also useful accessories.

Many lathe turners prefer to use heavy lathes so that vibrations are minimized. One can either purchase a heavy lathe, or weight the stand with sand, concrete, bricks, or other heavy materials.

Standing at the lathe is different than standing in front of a table saw or drill press. Because you are usually standing in one position for longer periods of time at the

Illus. 5-36. A Delta wood shaper. This shaper has a double-ended ½- and ¾-inch spindle, a 1½-horsepower motor, a reversing switch, and runs to 7,000 and 10,000 rpm.

Illus. 5-37. A Delta 12-inch wood lathe with variable speeds.

Illus. 5-38. A Delta 16-inch electronic variable-speed wood lathe. It includes the following: a 16-inch swing over the bed, a 24-inch outboard swing, a 53-inch distance between centers, forward speeds of 300–2,200 rpm, and reverse speeds of 300–1,000 rpm. It weighs 485 pounds.

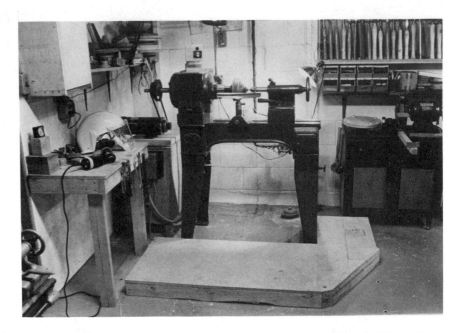

Illus. 5-39. This customized lathe has a shortened bed and raised head stock to accommodate larger bowl turnings, and a direct-current motor with variable speeds of 0–1,500 rpm that is mounted on the out-board shaft.

lathe, comfort is an important consideration. If you have to bend over the lathe, the consequences can be a sore neck or back. To compensate, you can stand on rubber mats and/or raise the lathe several inches off the floor. If you decide to raise the lathe, be certain that both the lathe and spacer block are firmly anchored to the main floor.

The lathe shown in Illus. 5-39 is unique in that Tom Zumbach, a lathe turner, has both shortened the lathe bed and raised the head stock so that he can turn larger bowls. The lathe is also fitted with a 1½-horsepower, variable-speed Baldor motor that operates in the range of 0 to 1,500 rpms (specifically, it is a silicon-controlled rectifier, direct-current motor). The head stock was raised by installing a spacer block. To compensate for the increased height of the work area, Tom built a platform for standing. The additional advantage of the platform is that it is more comfortable than concrete flooring. Also note the Airstream helmet, the right-angle drill for sanding, the two work lamps, the storage space for tools on the wall, and the proximity of the grinder for sharpening.

Drill Presses

The drill press provides a degree of control and accuracy impossible to achieve with a hand drill alone (Illus. 5-40). Holes can be drilled to specific sizes, and, if a fence is added to the table of a drill press, straight rows of holes can be routinely drilled. Stop devices can be attached to the table fence so that multiple workpieces can be posi-

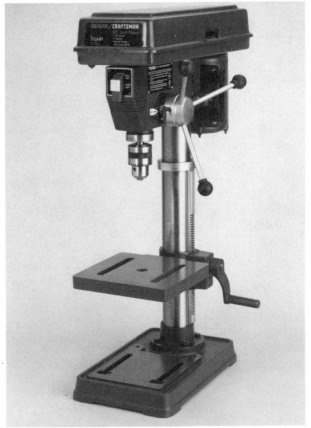

Illus. 5-40. This Sears 10-inch bench drill press has a ½-horsepower motor, a ½-inch chuck, and 4 speeds from 480 to 3,000 rpm.

tioned in the same place, in order to drill holes accurately and consistently.

There are two basic drill presses: floor and table models. The floor model provides more space between the drill chuck and the table. Table models are popular for smaller work or where floor space is at a minimum.

Drill presses are available in a range of sizes. A 16-inch drill press has a column-to-chuck distance of 8 inches; that is, you can drill in the center of a 16-inch-wide board. Drill presses are available with motors ranging from ¼ to 1 horsepower. A ¾-horsepower motor is adequate for most applications. The drilling speeds on most machines can be varied from 200 to 3,000 rpm by changing the belt positions on the pulleys. For most applications, slower speeds are recommended for large-diameter cutters and hard materials.

A variety of drill bits is very important. The standard twist bits are fine for metal, but generally produce poor results in wood because the wood fibres tend to tear instead of being cleanly severed. Drilling in wood is best done with brad-point, spade, Forstner and multispur bits. All of these bits have a sharp center point and some type of cutting edge around their circumference. These drill bits are available in sizes ranging from ¹⁄₁₆ inch to over 3 inches in diameter.

Accessories which enhance the use of the drill press include auxiliary fences, hold-down or clamping devises, sanding drums, wire brushes, mortising attachments, safety guards (Illus. 5-41), and gooseneck lamps.

Illus. 5-41. A Biesemeyer T-square drill press guard.

Illus. 5-42. This Delta 16½-inch drill press has a ⅝-inch chuck, 12 speeds from 250 to 3,000 rpm, and a ¾-horsepower motor. The drill table is mounted with a Jointer's Edge fence and positional stops.

The table and fence shown in Illus. 5-42 have several notable features. A piece of plywood with a solid wood edge (for wear resistance) is secured to the smaller metal table furnished with the drill press. The Jointer's Edge fence can be located anywhere on the table, and is secured by two threaded blocks which fit into the lower-surface T slot of the fence. When the knobs are tightened, they clamp the fence at the table's edge. There are two types of stop blocks on the fence: a simple wooden block and a metal stop with a spring-engaged stop finger. Both can be attached to either the top or front-side T slots of the fence. A magnet on the side of the drill press keeps the chuck key handy.

Hand Drills

Hand drills are a very popular portable power tool (Illus. 5-43). Sanding and wire-brushing are well suited to the hand-held drill. However, these drills have limited usefulness for drilling holes for woodworking projects if they are not used with a jig. It is difficult to hand-hold a drill and make a perfectly round hole. It is more likely that you will drill an oval-shaped hole that is not perpendicular to the wood surface. Fortunately, many different types of drilling jigs are available to match both your budget and needs.

Illus. 5-44. A Skil ⅜-inch variable-speed, reversing drill kit with a 12-volt battery and 1-hour battery charger.

Illus. 5-43. Sears Industrial variable-speed, reversing ½-inch drills.

Cordless drills and screwdrivers are significant recent innovations (Illus. 5-44 an 5-45). The larger drills generally have 9- to 12-volt batteries and are capable of repetitive drilling in the hardest of woods. Battery chargers are usually provided with the drill, and some units can recharge a depleted battery in less than one hour. The

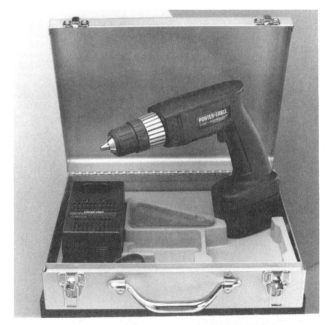

Illus. 5-45. A Porter Cable variable-speed, reversing drill with keyless chuck, 12-volt battery, and 1-hour battery charger.

Porter Cable drill also features a keyless chuck for quick-bit installation and removal.

Plate Joiners

Without a doubt, plate joiners are one of the most useful assembly tools in the shop (Illus. 5-46–5-49). The built-in front fence makes referencing the tool to the workpiece easy. When the plate joiner is in position, the cutter is pushed a set amount into the wood. If a matching board is cut in a similar fashion and a biscuit plate inserted into the slot, the boards will evenly fit against each other. If a frame-and-panel cabinet door takes 30 minutes to lay out, drill, and assemble with standard dowels, then the same assembly would take less than five minutes with a plate joiner, and the joints would be better aligned.

Biscuit plates are generally made of compressed beech that has the grain pattern diagonal to the biscuit's long axis. The diagonal grain pattern makes the biscuit more compatible with the grain direction of the workpiece. The compressed biscuit just fits into the slot, and then expands when in contact with glue.

Plate joiners can be used on edges, flat surfaces, beveled and angled pieces, and can also be used to cut long dadoes, grooves, and openings for special biscuit-shaped hinges and knock-down furniture fittings. Some plate joiners are available with dust-hose fittings or attached dust bags.

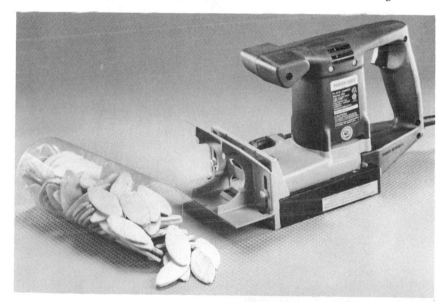

Illus. 5-46. A Porter Cable plate joiner with a container of biscuits.

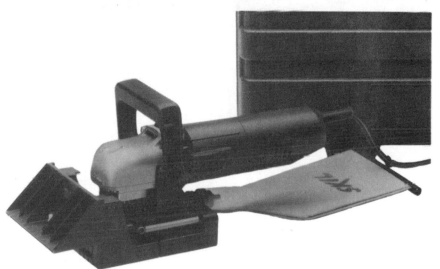

Illus. 5-47. A Skil plate joiner.

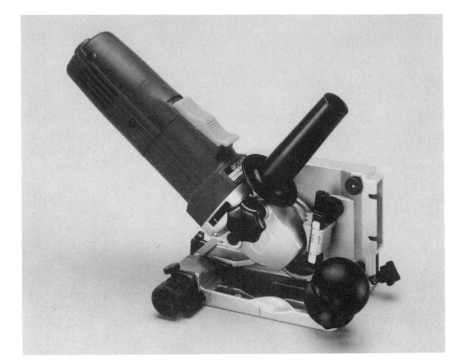

Illus. 5-48. An Elu jointer/spliner.

Illus. 5-49. A Delta plate joiner. This is a stationary tool with pedal control of the plunging action.

Scroll Saws

Scroll saws have become very popular in the last few years. No other power saw cuts as cleanly and as intricately, is so easy to use, or produces finished results that are as quickly seen (Illus. 5-50 and 5-51). Quality scroll saws can cut wood that is paper-thin or 2 inches thick.

Soft nonferrous metals and plastics can be cut if the saw has variable-speed capability. Blade stroke is the measured amount of up-and-down motion. Scroll saws with blade strokes of ⅝ to 1 inch are the most common.

The best blade for scroll saws is referred to as a "pinless" or plain-end blade. The blade is gripped, or fas-

Illus. 5-50. A Sears 16-inch variable-speed scroll saw.

Illus. 5-51. A Sears 20-inch variable-speed scroll saw.

tened, in a blade holder at the ends of the arms and tensioned until it can be plucked like a violin string. The blades have almost no set, are very thin, and are available in different sizes and teeth patterns for use with different materials and thicknesses of wood. The blade's tautness, fine size, and motion produces precise and intricate cuts.

The scroll-saw blades shown in Illus. 5-52 are from The Olson Saw Co. Specifications for the blades from left to right are shown in Chart 5-1.

Common accessories for scroll saws include an assortment of blades, lamps (sometimes with built-in magnifiers), and foot switches (Illus. 5-53).

Power Carving Tools

Power carving tools—sometimes referred to as power rotary tools—can be used to carve, grind, polish, sand, and engrave. They are available as either hand-held (Illus. 5-54) or flexible-shaft (Illus. 5-55 and 5-56) tools. Their motors range from 1 to 3 amps ($\frac{1}{15}$ to $\frac{1}{4}$ horsepower) and produce speeds of 5,000 to 30,000 rpm. Having selected the tool, the next step is to choose from the enormous variety of accessory cutters, points and burs. Suffice it to say that there are hundreds of bits designed for working wood, metal, jewelry, ceramics, glass, plastics, bone, fiberglass, rubber and stone, to name the most common materials.

Attachments which enhance the use of power carving

Illus. 5-52. A close-up of seven Olsen Saw Blade Company scroll-saw blades.

Chart 5-1.

Universal No.	Width	Thickness	TPI	Length
1	.026″	.013″	30	5″
2	.029″	.012″	20	5″
3	.032″	.014″	23	5″
5	.038″	.016″	12.5	5″
7	.044″	.018″	13	5″
9	.053″	.018″	11.5	5″
12	.061″	.022″	10	5″

Illus. 5-53. A Hegner scroll saw with an on/off foot switch.

Illus. 5-54. Dremel rotary hand tools. The older model on the right is fitted with a router attachment and custom-made Lexan base.

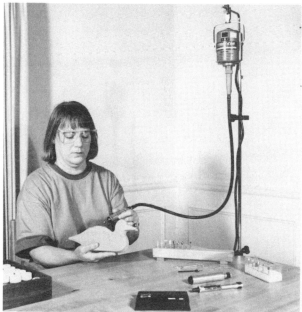

Illus. 5-55. This Foredom power tool can be used for many purposes, including wood carving. It is easily suspended from the accessory hanger and can be set up in a room work area. The unit has an 18,000 rpm, ⅛-horsepower motor. Its variable speeds are controlled with a foot switch. Different hand pieces are available.

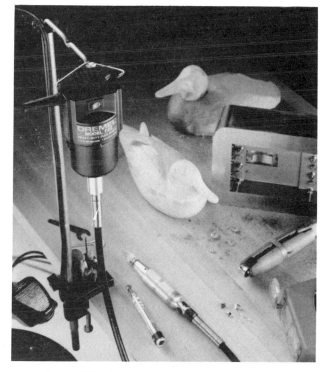

Illus. 5-56. This Dremel power tool has 20,000 rpm, a ⅕-horsepower motor and variable speeds that are controlled with a foot switch. Different hand pieces are available.

tools include a drill-press stand, a router base, a shaper table, vises, and holders. Accessories for flexible-shaft tools include different hand pieces (Illus. 5-57), foot-speed controls, motor hangers, hand-piece holders, and hand-piece grips.

Illus. 5-57. The Foredom power tool can be fitted with approximately 21 different hand pieces. Popular hand pieces are (from top to bottom) a geared three-jaw chuck, a slim hand piece with collets, a built-in chuck guard sleeve which slides near the chuck to protect fingers, and a hand piece with different-sized collets.

CHAPTER SIX

Combination Machines

The variety of tools, machines, and accessories from which one can choose is greater now than at any other time in history. Coupled with the variety of tools is an explosion of tool catalogues, magazines, videos and books. With the number of commercial products that are readily available from all these sources, it is possible to buy many single-purpose machines. These tools can be very efficient.

A practical alternative to single purpose machines are multi-purpose or combination machines. The combination machine can be composed of many different tools: table saw, jointer, planer, shaper, drill press, mortiser, sander, and lathe. Although some combination machines can be used for as many as five different functions, in this section machines that offer as few as two different functions are considered combination machines.

Combination machines are very popular in Europe, and European woodworkers have long used them as their principal machines. They are found in schools, small shops, and even production shops. In fact, many Europeans think of the combination machine as the optimal tool for woodworking. The combination machine is attractive because it offers affordability, versatility, maximization of work space, and centralization of the work environment.

Combination machines, however, require a more organized approach to the process of woodworking than is required with single-purpose machines. With single-purpose machines, you can use the table saw, walk over to the sander, return to the table saw, use the drill press, and finish at the sander. Work can seemingly be done in a random order (although being organized and having the work sequence planned out should be a goal regardless of whether one uses single-purpose or combination ma

chines). If you were using a combination machine as both a table saw and mortiser, repeatedly changing the elevation of the table saw to alternate between functions can affect the alignment of the mortise bit. In this situation, it would be prudent to make all cuts on the table saw before beginning the mortising work.

Some combination machines have tool functions which are complementary to each other. In some, the function of a tool has been compromised in order to integrate it into the machine, for example, a table saw's table that is too small to provide adequate support, or a lathe that is too lightweight for bowl turnings. Some tools in the combination machines are not useful in the general-purpose shop. Also, the process of changing from one tool function to another is easier with some combination machines than others. The biggest disadvantage concerning using combination machines is the interruptions caused by having to disassemble the machine in order to switch from one function to another.

Combination machines should be judged according to whether they have the appropriate tool functions, whether they can be changed easily from one function to another, and the quality of the individual tool functions. Combination machines which have similar functions, such as the belt/disc sanding machine or the jointer/planer, can prove more helpful.

A Sampling of Combination Machines

Below are the basic features and specifications for eight combination machines: the Robland X31 (Illus. 6-1), the Kity K5 (Illus. 6-2), the Kity 609Ti, the Kity 638, the Kity 652, the Shopsmith Mark 500 and Mark V 510 (Illus. 6-3), and the Felder BF6 26 (Illus. 6-4).

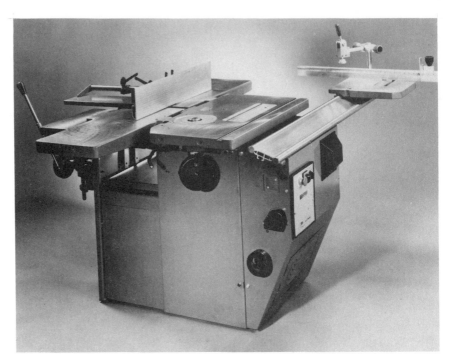

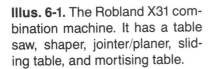

Illus. 6-1. The Robland X31 combination machine. It has a table saw, shaper, jointer/planer, sliding table, and mortising table.

Illus. 6-2. The Kity K-5 combination machine. It has a table saw, jointer/planer, shaper, and a mortising table.

Illus. 6-3. The Shopsmith Mark V, model 510 combination machine. Here it is set up as a table saw, but it can be converted to a lathe, horizontal boring machine, disc sander, and drill press.

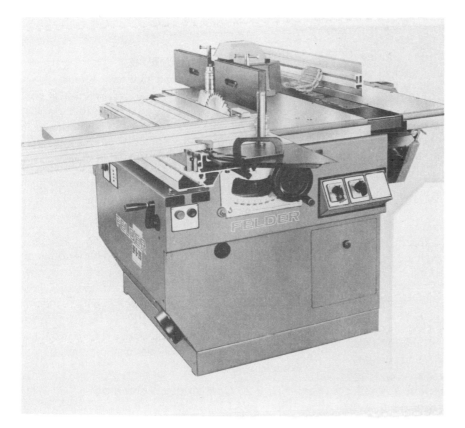

Illus. 6-4. The Felder model BF6-26 combination machine. It has a table saw, shaper, sliding table, and jointer/planer.

Illus. 6-5. This Kity combination machine has a table saw, shaper, jointer/planer, and sliding table.

Robland X31 Combination Machine

The Robland combination machine contains the following: a jointer/planer with a 12-inch-knife length, a tilting-arbor table saw with a 10-inch saw blade, a shaper with ¾- and 1¼-inch-diameter spindles, a mortiser with a ⅝-inch-capacity chuck, and a sliding table. It has a separate 20-amp, 3-horsepower, 220-volt motor for the table saw, shaper, and jointer/planer. It weighs 1,100 pounds.

Kity K-5 Combination Machine

The Kity K-5 combination machine has the following: a jointer/planer that uses knives 6 inches long, a table saw that uses a blade 8 inches in diameter, a shaper that has a spindle ¾ inch in diameter, and a ⅜-inch-capacity mortiser. It has an 11 amp, 1½-horsepower, 110-volt motor, and weighs 168 pounds.

Kity 609Ti Combination Machine

The Kity 609Ti combination machine is a larger combination machine than the K-5. It can be customized to the specifications of the individual woodworker and contains the following: a tilting-arbor table saw that uses a 10-inch-diameter blade; a tilting-arbor shaper with a 30-mm spindle that operates at 4,800, 6,400 and 8,700 rpm; and a sliding table. It has a separate 2-horsepower, 1-phase,

220-volt motor for the table saw and shaper, and weighs 640 pounds.

Kity 638 Combination Machine

The Kity 638 combination machine has a jointer/planer that uses a 12½-inch-long knife and operates at a feed speed of 29 feet per minute. It has a 2½-horsepower, 1-phase, 220-volt motor and weighs 440 pounds.

Kity 652 Mortiser Machine

The Kity 652 Mortiser Machine has a table size of 7⅞ × 15¾ inches. It cuts mortises to a maximum length of 5 inches and maximum width of ⅝ inch.

Shopsmith Mark V 500 and Mark V 510 Combination Machines

The Shopsmith Mark V 500 and Mark V 510 combination machines have the following: a tilting-table table saw that uses a 10-inch-diameter saw blade, a drill press, a lathe with a distance of 34 inches between centers and 8⅛ inches over the bed, a horizontal borer with a 4½-inch quill travel, and a 12-inch disc sander. These machines have a 1⅛ horsepower, 110-volt motor, and weigh 205 and 252 pounds, respectively.

Felder BF6 26 Combination Machine

The Felder BF6 26 combination machine contains the following: a jointer/planer that uses a 10-inch-long knife;

a tilting-arbor table saw that accepts saw blades from 6 to 12 inches; a shaper with a 30-mm reversible tilting spindle that operates at speeds of 3,500, 6,100 and 7,800 rpm; and a crosscut sliding table. It has a separate 220-volt, 3-horsepower motor for the jointer/planer, table saw, and shaper, and weighs 510 kg.

Comparing Combination Machines
The Robland X31, Kity 609Ti, and the Felder BF6 26 combination machines are large units with several motors and powerful features. These machines are designed for the serious woodworking amateur and professional. Some woodworkers utilize them in shops with several employees or in shops where the machines are in continual use throughout the day. In these cases, the machines were deliberately chosen on the basis of their specifications and because the machine allows the work process to be centralized in one area. Changing over from one function to another is quick and simple, because of the excellent design qualities of these machines, which is further facilitated by the use of separate motors for the individual components.

The Kity K5 and Shopsmith Mark V are smaller than the other three machines. These machines are designed primarily for use in smaller shops; in fact, the Kity K5 can be used in a shop as small as 6 × 8 feet. The Kity K5 comes with casters and levelling feet; similar features are options for the Shopsmith Mark V. Both machines will fit through a 30-inch-wide door frame. The principal difference between the two machines is that it requires less time to change tool functions on the Kity K5 than the Shopsmith Mark V, because the shaper, table saw and jointer/planer work independently of each other. Changeover on the Kity K5 is confined to moving the drive belt, whereas the Shopsmith Mark V requires more extensive rearrangement of the machine to access the individual functions.

Jointer/Planers

Many woodworkers believe that the table saw or radial arm saw should be the first machine purchased for the shop. This may be true, but what if you need wood that is a specific thickness and is also smooth, flat, and free of twists, cups and bows? You cannot simply cut the thickness of a 10-inch-wide board on a saw.

There are two common methods for planing wood. In the first method, only a wide planer is used for wood preparation. The second method uses both a jointer and a planer. One disadvantage with the second method is that there are a variety of planers from 10 to 24 inches wide,

but few wide jointers. And the cost of the two individual machines can be prohibitive. A logical alternative to having a jointer and a planer is the combination jointer/planer.

Many manufacturers, retailers, and woodworkers seem to believe that the function and advantages of the jointer/planer are not well understood. Americans typically have seemed to resist the idea of using combination machines. However, the jointer/planer should not be thought of as the typical combination machine. It integrates functions that naturally belong together. A jointer/planer conserves space in the workshop; it is like having two machines, but only needing room for one. A jointer/planer is cost-effective; most jointer/planers cost significantly less than a jointer *and* a planer. But the real value of a combination jointer/planer is that you can do a better job of preparing wood.

When only planers are used, the board is fed into the machine to smooth its surface or reduce its thickness. But generally, any twists or bows in the board are not removed. So the board first has to be flattened with a hand plane or wide jointer. Hand planing is not for everyone, nor is it necessarily feasible when you are working on hundreds of board feet.

Skillful integration of the functions of jointing and planing is the key to resolving the problem of smoothing wood that is neither flat nor free of twists. The secret is rather simple: The same cutterhead and knives are used for both the planer and jointer functions. All you need to do is flatten the board on the jointer table, and then feed it under the same cutterhead for the planer work.

The jointer/planer also solves an important safety consideration. Rather than using the table saw to rip-cut a wide board so that it will fit on a narrow jointer, it is much better to flatten one side on the wide jointer before any rip cutting is done. Rip-cutting rough-surfaced wood is dangerous because wood with twists or cupping can cause kickback.

The first step in preparing wood using a jointer/planer is to flatten one side of the board on the jointer table. It takes practice to flatten a cupped, twisted, or bowed board, so at first you may find that all the planing is occurring at opposite or opposing corners of the board. If this continues, the ¼ (one-inch-thick) wood you bought will turn out thinner than ⅞-inch. However, this can be advantageous because it is much better to build furniture with flat wood. Joints, such as dovetails and finger joints, will fit and look better if the wood is flat and free of curved surfaces.

To facilitate the planing process, jointer/planers usually have smooth, roller-free planer tables. The wood is pulled to the cutterhead by a power-driven in-feed roller; usually the in-feed roller is either toothed or serrated. On the other side of the cutterhead is a smooth out-feed roller that is also power driven. Once one surface is flat, either one or both of the jointer tables can be pivoted or removed for access to the planer. Usually this takes only a few seconds, and the jointer/planer is ready to start planing again.

A Sampling of Jointer/Planer Machines

The following are the cutter sizes (knife lengths) of several jointer/planer machines whose working capacity ranges from 10 to 16 inches. The *Inca model 550* machine has a 10¼-inch cutter. The *model 570* machine has a 10¼-inch cutter. The *Kity model 638* machine has a 12⅛-inch cutter. The *Mini Max model FS35* machine has a 12-inch cutter. The *model FS31* machine has a 13½-inch cutter. The *Robland model XSD31* machine has a 12³⁄₁₆-inch cutter. The *Felder model BF5 41AD* machine has a 16-inch cutter.

Inca Models 550 and 570 Jointer/Planer Machines The difference between the Inca model 550 and 570 machines

Illus. 6-7. The Inca model 550 jointer/planer with out-feed table removed to reveal the planer table.

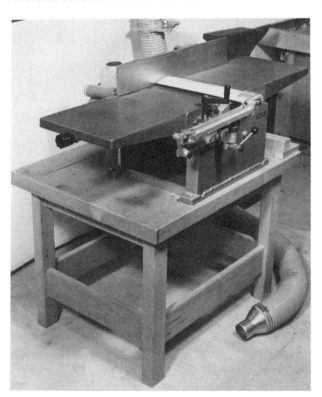

Illus. 6-6. The Inca model 550 jointer/planer. It is mounted on a custom-made stand.

is the cutterhead. The Inca 570 has a Tersa cutterhead with three disposable/reversible tool steel knives. The Inca 550 (Illus. 6-6 and 6-7) has a two-knife cutterhead and its high-speed steel (HSS) blades are changed and sharpened in a standard fashion, with the exception that there are slots in the knives for the flange end of the adjustment screws. This facilitates knife adjustment either up or down when it is in the cutterhead.

To change the Inca 570 knives, tap on the backing bar with a small block of wood and a hammer to loosen both the backing bar and the knife. Slide the knife out to the side of the cutterhead, and then slide in the new knife. There is nothing to tighten or align. Just turn the machine on and centrifugal force will align and lock up the knife. It takes about 45 seconds to change the three knives.

To change from jointing to planing is a simple three-step procedure: move the fence to the side of the tables, completely remove the out-feed jointer table from the machine, and snap the dust-collector attachment over the cutterhead. The whole process takes about a minute. It is easy to remove and install the table, and the table can be realigned perfectly when it is repositioned. Inca jointer table adjustments are easy to make. These jointers have a centered-to-the-table adjustment knob requiring no locking device.

Inca machines have the slowest feed-rate speeds of the machines listed, but they are the only machines with two speeds: 11.5 and 16.5 feet/minute. These speeds, and a neutral position, can be changed via a lever during operation. The planer scale is reversible and scaled in both inches and millimeters. The jointer bed height scale is a nonindicated, relative scale. One turn of the planer height-adjustment handle equals 3/32 inch. Inca jointer/planers do not have a center column support for the planer surface. Instead, there is a chain-drive system with adjustment posts at the four corners of the planer table.

The Inca jointer/planers are not very heavy (only 125 pounds), so they can be easily moved and transported. The tables of the Inca jointer/planers are made of cast and anodized aluminum; however, the surface of the planer bed is stainless steel. The fence is unremarkable and somewhat short, although it is effective. Inca jointer/planers don't come with bases, although you can buy an accessory wooden table or make one yourself.

Kity Model 638 Jointer/Planer The Kity 638 jointer/planer (Illus. 6-8) is comfortable to use, and the extruded aluminum fence extends the full length of the jointer. The fence adjustment is simple, but slightly awkward for left-handers. The knives are disposable and reversible, but

they are set and adjusted in the cutterhead like standard knives.

Changing the Kity 638 from the jointer to the planer requires that the fence be removed from the machine; then both jointer tables must be released by lever on one side so that they can be pivoted to the opposite side. The dust collector is then moved over the cutterhead. With the exception of having to remove the fence, the change-over process is easy and quick.

The control knob for raising or lowering the table is part of the pivot point. The other side of the table rests upon the frame near the locking lever for the table. If you attempt to adjust the table height when the hold-down lever is tightened, the table will move in a skewed fashion. To remedy this, keep the locking-lever in place, but not tight.

The feed rate of the Kity 638 is 29 feet/minute. The jointer bed and planer height scales are in inches. One turn of the planer adjustment handle moves the planer table 1/8 inch.

A nice feature of the Kity 638 is the interconnected electrical switches at either end of the machine which allow the machine to be turned off and on from either of the working locations. The Kity machine is also electrically interlocked via micro-switches at the pivot points, which ensures that the machine will only run when all guards are in their correct position.

The Kity jointer/planer, like the Inca jointer/planer,

Illus. 6-8. The Kity model 638 jointer/planer.

has an anodized aluminum table. But unlike the Inca machines, the Kity machine has a built-on base unit. A particularly unique feature of the Kity 638 is its removable angle-iron bars which fit to either side of the base for lifting the machine, even with a forklift.

Mini Max Models FS31 and FS35 Jointer/Planers The visible differences between the Mini Max models FS31 and FS35 (Illus. 6-9) jointer/planers are weight, jointer bed size, and knife length (12 and 13½ inches, respectively).

Illus. 6-9. The Mini-Max model FS35 jointer/planer. The jointer tables are raised to reveal the planer table.

Both Mini Max machines use the standard type of knives and have cast-iron, surface-ground tables. Instead of round extraction ports, the Mini Max jointer/planers have dust-removal chutes. The planer height scale and jointer table scale are in both inches and metric.

Using the Mini Max as a jointer is straightforward, although the fence is short and somewhat difficult to use because an Allen wrench is needed to adjust the fence angle. To use the planer, both tables are released by

simple locks; then the tables are pivoted, and the dust chute is positioned over the cutterhead. Only a few seconds is required to change between functions, even though the tables are very heavy.

To avoid table misalignment, the Mini Max models incorporate a sliding plate which interlocks into grooves in both gibb ways. A single lever moves the plate when adjustments are being made in table height. While there is play in the table when the locking mechanism is loose, the table pulls straight when locked.

Robland Model XSD-31 Jointer/Planers The Robland XSD-31 jointer/planer is a well-made jointer/planer that is solid, balanced, and not top-heavy. As a jointer, it is easy to use for working wide and long pieces of wood. Each table can be raised or lowered via conveniently placed adjustment knobs. The tables have no scales to indicate depth of cut. The power switches for jointing are well laid out, although they are positioned a bit low for easy reach. Another easier-to-reach switch which is used for the planer operation is on the opposite, diagonal corner.

The tall, extruded aluminum fence is easy to use because of a unique, articulated tilting mechanism which also has positive stops at 45 and 90 degrees. Like the Inca jointer/planers, the Robland fence is shorter than I prefer, but it created no work problems.

To change to the planer, simple cam-lock levers are

Illus. 6-10. The Robland XSD-31 jointer/planer.

used to release each table, and then the well-balanced tables smoothly pivot to the side. The fence does not have to be removed or adjusted in order to pivot the tables. The side opposite the pivot points has flat bolt heads for the table to slide upon. These heads are also used to adjust the table if it's out of alignment. Once the dust extraction unit is positioned over the cutterhead, the planer/jointer is ready to use.

The feed rate of the Robland planer/jointer is 19 feet/minute. It is slightly faster than the Inca machines, but slower than the other machines. The three knives are held in the cutterhead, in the typical fashion, with a backing bar and nuts on tightening screws. The Robland jointer/planer also has a device for setting the knives.

Felder Model BF541 AD Jointer/Planer The Felder model BF541 AD jointer/planer is perhaps the most sophisticated of the jointer/planers, and is especially useful in a production shop. It is the heaviest (970 pounds), widest (16 inches), and most expensive of the machines listed. Among its notable features are electrical switches mounted on a post at eye level and table extensions which add an additional 40 inches to the jointer table and provide a 43-inch total length to the planing surface. To speed up blade changing and ensure cutting accuracy, four disposable/reversible high-speed steel knives are secured with hex screws in factory-set gibbs. The Felder jointer/planer comes with a 3-phase, 4-horsepower motor. (Many Felder owners use a rotary phase converter if their shop doesn't have 3-phase power.)

The jointer tables pivot on one side, and are secured and locked on the operator's side. The tables rest on machined surfaces. The height of the tables can be adjusted by loosening the locking lever, which allows the table to be moved freely. All the locking levers for the table and fence are engaged via an eccentric cam-lock system and are simple to use.

Comparing Jointer/Planers Several key points to consider as you prepare to buy a jointer/planer are the type and volume of use, the width capacity of the machine, your expectation for the quality of the planed surface, and cost. Planer feed rate is an important criterion if you plan to joint and plane hundreds of board feet, as opposed to preparing smaller quantities. The number of cuts per inch will determine whether you get minimal tear-out on high-grade wood. Also consider the machine's weight and the weight and balance of the jointer tables, especially as regards moving them, and your preference for using disposable knives (which do not require sharpening) or reusable knives.

The *Felder model BF541 AD* jointer/planer is an expensive, yet effective machine. Using a 16-inch jointer and planer is very helpful, and the disposable/reversible 16-inch knives ensure straight-knife edges. Table extensions can be added to both jointer tables; the planer out-feed table extension is especially helpful. The fence is sturdy and easy to adjust. The electrical switches are located up in the air. The jointer tables are well balanced at the pivot points and easily moved for access to the planer. The planer produces good-quality wood surfaces with light knife markings.

The *Inca model 550 and 570* jointer/planers have the slowest feed rates, but the number of cuts per inch minimizes tear-out and produces beautiful glassy finishes, even on bird's-eye maple. These are ideal machines for musical instrument makers and for those making one-of-a-kind furniture pieces. Despite the machines' short jointer bed and planer surface, they are able to handle $2 \times 9 \times 80$-inch oak planks. The jointer tables on these machines are extremely flat—within .004 inch from end to end. The disposable/reversible knives are very effective. It takes less than a minute to change all three. The knives have two edges, and several woodworkers have told me that they do most of their work with one edge and use the reverse edges to make the final smoothing cuts. The Inca models do not offer an accessory mortising table. Both models are lightweight and can easily be moved into a basement shop.

The *Kity model 638* jointer/planer is a good choice for the home workshop or busy one-person shop. Although it weighs only 440 pounds, it has the look and feel of a machine twice the weight. And the 12½-inch knive it uses is a good size for most needs. The Kity is comfortable to use. The dual electrical switches are especially helpful. One drawback is that the fence has to be removed in order to use the planer. Fence removal does not take long, but you need a convenient storage place for it. The Kity has the fastest feed rate at 29 feet/minute. The wood surfaces are very high quality; only light cut marks are visible.

The *Mini Max model FS35* jointer/planer would work fine in either the busy home shop or medium-sized production shop. Its most noticeable features are the 13½-inch knives it uses, heavy jointer tables, its fence design, and the adjustment levers for the jointer tables. The table length and knife size make it easy to work very large pieces of wood. The tables are very heavy, so use care when lifting them between jointer and planer functions. If the tables do go out of alignment, they can be reset via blocks on the main frame. Also, the jointer adjustment levers take time to learn to use. This jointer/planer will be better served if it had a round hook-up port for dust extraction and a better jointer table scale. The Mini Max FS35 produces satisfactory wood surfaces with lightly cut marks.

The *Robland model XSD31* jointer/planer is an easy-to-use machine which produces excellent wood surfaces. The jointer/planer is actually one part of the Robland X31 combination machine; the other part is the shaper and table saw unit. The 12 × 55-inch jointer table works nicely in either the home or commercial shop. Both tables are easy to raise or lower when jointing, and are very well balanced when you are changing over for planing. The cam-locking levers securing the tables are also quick and easy to use. The fence is easy to adjust and does not have to be moved out of the way when the tables are being pivoted.

Mortising Attachments

The mortising chuck is generally driven off the cutterhead, so it is right in the middle of any work activity. This means that if the mortiser is mounted to the back side of the machine, you can't place the jointer/planer against a wall. If the mortiser is on the operator side, then it should be removed, especially when jointing, because it is in the way.

Machine Adaptations

Unless you are doing production work and all the shop machines are constantly in use, most machines in the workshop at some time will not be in use. It's not uncommon to use the radial arm saw to cut workpieces to length at the start of a project, and then only infrequently for the remainder of the work cycle. The following are adaptations that have been made to machines to better utilize them.

Monty Parker primarily makes lathe turnings and, as a consequence, his jointer/planer, band saw, and shaper are sitting idle for periods of time. He made plywood covers for these machines so that they could be used as flat storage surfaces for odds and ends. The plywood covers protect and conceal cutterheads, table slots, and other openings. The covers also keep dirt, liquids, and items that scratch from marring machine tops (Illus. 6-11 and 6-12).

The router table shown in Illus. 6-13 and 6-14 has a ¾-inch-diameter hole drilled through it so that the universal vise can be attached to it. There is also a wooden space block used to raise the vise to a higher and more comfortable working height.

Jim Kirchner has a small shop in which he makes musical instruments. One of the larger machines in his

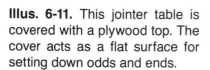

Illus. 6-11. This jointer table is covered with a plywood top. The cover acts as a flat surface for setting down odds and ends.

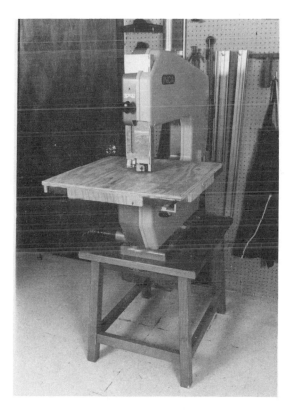

Illus. 6-12. The table on this band saw is covered with a plywood top which acts as an extra surface for temporarily placing small items.

Illus. 6-13. A view of a shop with pegboard wall storage. Note that the router table can also be used to secure a universal vise.

Illus. 6-14. A close-up of the router table and disassembled universal vise.

Illus. 6-15. A shop-made oscillating sander.

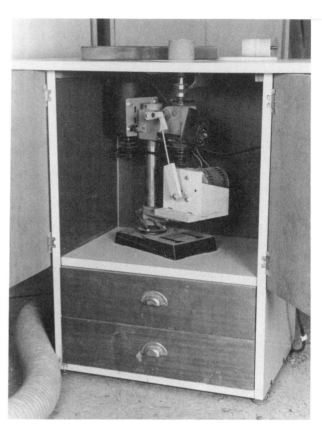

Illus. 6-16. An inside view of a small drill press that has been modified into an oscillating sander.

Illus. 6-17. The oscillating sander is used in a small shop where space is at a premium. When the sander is not in use, the table is used for other functions. A bending iron is clamped to the table for bending thin strips of wood.

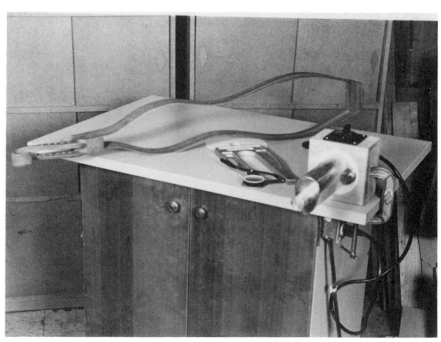

shop is a shop-made oscillating drum sander, which he made from a small drill press (Illus. 6-15 and 6-16). The sander has different-sized sanding drums and table inserts to accommodate the various curves associated with harps and other instruments. However, since the sander is not in constant use, the machine top is used for other functions. In Illus. 6-17, an electric bending iron for heat-bending thin wood is clamped to the table's edge. Cal-

ipers and workpieces are then accessible on the tabletop while work is being done.

The sander top is also used as a surface for veneer clamps, as shown in Illus. 6-18. The clamps do not need a special device to hold them in position, because they are heavy and stable enough for clamping on top of the sander, and when they are not in use they are stored away in a corner of the shop.

Illus. 6-18. The sander tabletop is used to support veneer clamp frames.

CHAPTER SEVEN

Dust Collection

Over the last 15 years, the importance of dust collectors for the small workshop has become increasingly recognized. At one time, it was not uncommon to see mounds of chips and dust piled around table saws, band saws, jointers and planers. Shops were hazy with dust, and the last part of the workday was devoted to shovelling and sweeping.

Now, dust collectors are being utilized more and more in small workshops. This is because wood dust is now recognized as a health, safety, and fire hazard. There are government regulations concerning the removal of wood dust. The Occupational Safety and Health Administration (OSHA) in the United States has ruled that if one or more persons are employed in a workshop, an employer must either have dust-control methods in place to limit the levels of dust in the air or provide approved filtered-breathing devices. Effective December 1992, breathing devices will no longer be permitted, and dust-control methods must be used.

Anyone who works in a home shop will benefit from these regulations and the increased awareness of dust as a potential health hazard. As information on health hazards is more widely available, so also has there been more of a selection of products for dust collecting.

There are many health risks associated with wood dust. Dust and chips are most likely to directly affect your eyes, skin, and respiratory system. Glasses or goggles can protect you against flying debris, but won't prevent dust from settling on your skin or in your lungs.

While sensitivity to dust varies from person to person, the variety of materials that we cut and make into dust also creates different concerns. Domestic wood, imported exotic woods, man-made materials, pesticides, and preservatives have unique chemical properties that should be kept away from the skin and the respiratory system. The health problems that some woods can cause are well documented. Western or Canadian red cedar causes problems that can develop into asthma or inflammation of the nasal passages. Redwood dust is the cause of sequoiosis, an illness that resembles pneumonia. Cocobolo dust can cause allergic (skin) dermatitis. Wood dust can cause other health problems, including irritation of the upper respiratory tract, inflammation of the nasal tract, tightness of the chest, shortness of breath, dizziness, asthma, rhinitis, mucosal irritations, numbness, fibrosis, contact dermatitis, conjunctivitis, itching and rashes.

Wood dust is also a fire hazard when it is loose and allowed to accumulate on the floor or machinery. Smoking or other sparking sources can ignite loose dust. Even dust that is in a storage container can ignite if a metal object (e.g., screw or nail) is drawn through the metal collector and causes a spark to hit the contained dust. To add one more consideration, if dust is in the right proportion to air and is ignited with a spark, an explosion can result. This can happen either within a room or within a dust-collection system. Dust should be stored in fireproof or fire-resistant containers and should be disposed of on a regular basis. (Electrostatic fire hazards will be described in the context of the various types of collector ducts.)

Until recently, shop vacuums were the most commonly used tools for cleaning shops. Although both shop vacuums and dust collectors can remove dust from the workshop, which can be deposited into a storage container, dust collectors can more effectively gather dust and larger particles. The minimum air flow for most woodworking tools is 300 to 700 CFM (cubic feet per minute). Home or shop vacuums can provide about 100 to 120 CFM. In contrast, dust collectors are capable of providing about 300 to 2,000 CFM. This means that dust and larger particles can be more efficiently transported through the collector hoses or pipes when a dust collector is used. Also, most shop vacuums do not have large enough storage containers or hoses for the volumes of dust that woodworking tools create.

When deciding which type of dust collector to use and where to locate it, first determine which of the shop machinery will be attached to the collector system. Next, compare the technical specifications of different dust collectors and select the one which has the best features for your needs. For example, a one-horsepower collector which produces 400 cfm (cubic feet per minute) is adequate for use with a single machine when its hose length is approximately 6 feet. But this unit is not powerful enough to be connected to several feet of duct or many machines.

There are two basic dust-collector designs for the home and small shop: single- and two-stage designs. Single-stage collectors draw all the dust and chips through the impeller housing. Debris then settles in a lower bag, and air is returned through a top-mounted filter bag. This is the most common collector, and its design does not vary significantly from manufacturer to manufacturer.

Unlike the single-stage collector, dust and chips are drawn into the two-stage collector so that the heavier particles settle into a drum and the finer dust is collected in a filter bag. This system is the safer of the two, because it is designed so that solid objects do not go through the impeller fan. Also, should a metal object be accidentally drawn into the collector, the chance of damage or sparks is minimized.

Before deciding upon a particular dust-collection system, there are several technical terms with which you should become familiar. *Air volume* is the amount of air moved through the duct and is measured in cubic feet per minute (cfm). *Air velocity* (or the speed of air through the duct) must be great enough to keep dust in suspension and avoid clogging the duct. It is measured in feet per minute (fpm). *Static pressure* is the resistance to air at rest in a duct (commonly referred to as pressure loss). *Velocity pressure* is the kinetic pressure in the direction of flow that is necessary to cause air at rest to flow at a specific velocity.

Also, verify that the dust collector's specifications are compatible with the duct system as regards duct diameter, length of duct work, amount of smoothness within the duct system, types of fittings (45- and 90-degree elbows, reducers, etc.), and number of machines and their respective cfm. All of these features directly affect the efficiency of a dust collector. No matter how powerful

the collector, choosing incorrect accessories will reduce the overall efficiency of the collection system.

Some conditions that can reduce the cfm rate inside a duct, perhaps so drastically that dust can barely be moved, are: a duct run that is too long, too many elbows or bends, a duct or hose that has a rough inside-wall surface, or a Y connector to another machine that is installed without a blast gate.

Dust can be collected into a cloth bag, plastic bag, or drum. Each type of container has its merits and limitations. A bag or drum of sawdust is heavy and awkward to handle. Determine whether the container can be emptied easily, cleanly and conveniently when it is full. Also, make sure that the bag does not come off the collector unless you remove it.

Attached plastic bags are not the most common type of collection bag, but they are the easiest to use for getting rid of dust. Simply take the plastic bag off the collector and throw it out with the trash. (Many cities and counties have new regulations concerning the disposal of different

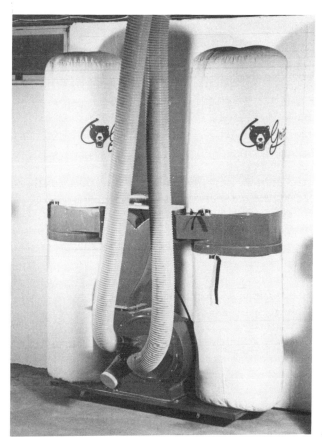

Illus. 7-1. The Grizzly Co. dust collector with four cloth bags.

Illus. 7-2. The Sears portable dust collector fitted to a small band saw.

types of trash. It is advisable to check with local authorities on how best to get rid of sawdust.)

Cloth bags are probably the most common type fitted to collectors (Illus. 7-1). Cloth bags are easy to use, but they are awkward to handle, especially when you have to dump the bag into something else. Also, check the owner's manual regarding the best method for cleaning the bags. Some companies recommend that the bags occasionally be laundered, while others suggest that the bags be shaken or not cleaned at all.

A second limitation of cloth bags is that some are so thin and porous that fine dust blows through them and back into the shop. An efficient, high-quality bag is available from the Delta Corp., which is described by the company as having a three-dimensional weave for dust retention.

Another limitation of cloth bags is the manner in which they are attached to the dust collector. There is the possibility that they will fall off the dust collector while you are using the tool it is attached to. It is essential that the retaining strap or clamp keep the bags securely on the collector while the collector is in use, yet be easy to operate when you are putting on or removing the bags. The Sears Craftsman model 29978 portable dust collector (Illus. 7-2) has one of the more effective adjustable band clamps for the upper bag. It also has an equally good system for attaching the lower bag. A metal hoop sewn into the open end of the lower bag is placed inside the collector housing and fits against a retaining surface. To remove the bag, you just push the hoop upwards and then compress it to lower the bag through the collector housing. If the bags on your collector are held on with drawstrings, you may want to replace them with large band clamps available at some hardware stores.

The dust-collector system manufactured by Delta Corp. is very effective because of the two-stage design of the collector (Illus. 7-3). Its only limitation is that the drum, which collects the large dust particles and chips,

Illus. 7-3. Delta models 50-181 and 50-179 dust collectors. The 50-181 sits on a 55-gallon fibre drum and the 50-179 sits on a Delta 35-gallon drum.

has to be emptied in some fashion. This means you either have to pick the drum up or tip it over to get the dust out.

An attractive alternative to the drum is to make an equivalent container out of wood. Construct a wooden box, cut a circular hole in its top, and make a raised lip of curved wood strips around the hole. At the base of the box, make a door that opens like a flap that is wide enough for a shovel to fit through. Be certain the door is properly sealed and secured when it is closed. As an extra precaution, paint the inside with fire-resistant paint. When the box gets full, simply open the door and empty the dust from the box with a shovel!

As you consider your choices of dust collectors, be sure to find out how noisy the collector is. The relative size of the collector is no indication. My first collector, which

was manufactured by a first-rate tool company, was small and extremely loud. In fact, it was so loud that I had to wear hearing protection just to work around it. The next one I bought was less expensive, and very quiet. Ask about the decibel level of the collector. Companies that make a quiet unit know the decibel level for their product, and will not be reluctant to tell you about it.

Dust Collectors

Chart 7-1 briefly summarizes the specifications of several commercially available dust collectors. It is by no means complete, but is intended to serve as an initial reference. (The Sears Craftsman model 29978 and the Delta model 50-179 dust-collectors are particularly well suited for smaller shops. Both are quiet, efficient units.)

Mfg.	Sears	Delta	Delta	Delta	SECO	Grizzly	Bridgewood
Model No.	29978	50-179	50-180	50-181	UFO-101	G1030	BW-003
Type (stages)	single	two	two	two	single	single	single
Motor	1	¾	1	2	2	3	3
Voltage	120	115/230	115/230	230	110/220	110/220	220
Amperes	7	10.6/5.3	13.6/6.8		24/12	36/18	16
CFM (max)	408	580	700	1,100	1,182	1,883	1,950
Static Press		7″	4.5″	8.5″	9″	6″	5.8″
dBA @ 5ft			83	85		75-95	
Hose Diameter	4″	4″	5″	6″	5″	4″	4″
# Hose Outlets	1	1	1	1	2	3	4
Bag Area (sq ft)	11	11	19	19	5.24 cu. ft		73.4
Bag Capacity (gal)		11.5	∅	∅	∅	≈3	144
Drum Size (gal)	∅	35	55	55	∅	∅	∅

Chart 7-1.

Pipes, Hoses, and Ducts

The efficiency of a dust collector is affected by the inside smoothness, durability, and air tightness of the hose, duct, or pipe. But not all hoses, pipes, and ducts are the same. There are many types to choose from. They are described below.

Plastic Pipe

Plastic pipe (PVC) is often used for dust collectors because it is easy to install, easy to seal and make airtight, and is readily available at the local hardware store. One disadvantage of using plastic pipe is the danger of static discharges within the pipe. A static discharge that occurs when dry air and dust are in a closed pipe is a potential hazard. If you use plastic pipe, make sure the pipe is properly grounded. To provide a ground, place a bare ground wire within the pipe from each tool to a ground connection at the dust collector. The wire should be tightly stretched against the bottom of the pipe so that wood chips do not become lodged within the pipe. If static electricity is produced despite this precaution, wrap another ground wire around the outside of the pipe in a spiral and attach it to the other ground wire. Illus. 7-4 shows how the grounding wire is spirally wrapped around plastic irrigation pipe (this has a thinner wall than plastic plumbing pipe). This particular setup is used to collect dust and debris from a lathe. When the lathe is not

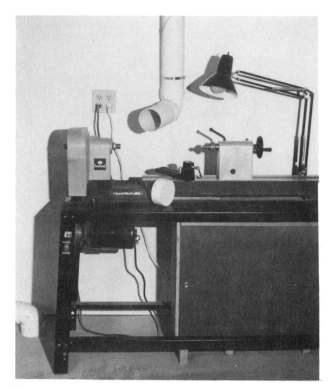

Illus. 7-4. Irrigation PVC pipe configured to act as a dust pick-up at a lathe. Note the grounding wire wrapped spirally around the pipe.

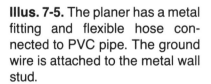

Illus. 7-5. The planer has a metal fitting and flexible hose connected to PVC pipe. The ground wire is attached to the metal wall stud.

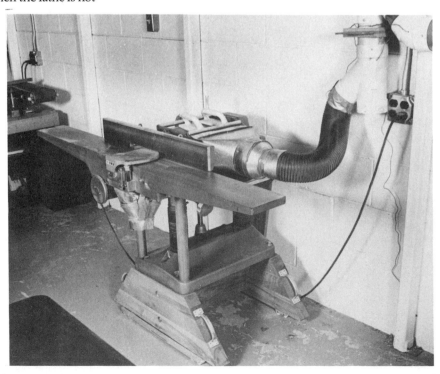

in use, the elbow is removed and a cap is placed on the end of the pipe.

Illus. 7-5 shows PVC pipe being used with a flexible hose that is connected to a sheet-metal fitting on the planer. Note that a grounding wire is attached to the metal wall stud.

Metal Pipe

Metal pipe has excellent features for dust collection, and is widely available in the form of standard sheet-metal furnace pipe, spiral galvanized pipe, and flexible metal hose (Illus. 7-6). There are also a variety of fittings, connectors and blast gates (Illus. 7-7) from which to choose. Illus. 7-8 shows a floor sweep (left) and a funnel-shaped fitting (right). The funnel-shaped piece could be used on a lathe or drill press. Metal pipe has smooth inside surfaces, can be easily grounded, and resists damage from dust and chips. But metal pipe is more expensive and difficult to install than plastic pipe. It has to be suspended with hangers, the male/female fittings have to correctly oriented to the direction of air flow, and the joints sealed with silicone sealer. (It is much harder to seal metal pipes for airtightness than plastic pipes.)

Flexible Hose

Flexible hose is another alternative. However, it should not be used for long runs, because the corregated shape of the inside creates some resistance to air and dust flow. Some flexible hoses are easily abraded by large wood pieces moving through the hose, or torn when they are accidentally nicked by a board or tool edge. Some flexible hoses have wire reinforcement which also acts as a

Illus. 7-6. A selection of different metal pipes, connectors, and fittings from Air Handling Systems Manufacturers Service Co.

Illus. 7-7. Assorted blast gates from Air Handling Systems Manufacturers Service Co.

Illus. 7-8. A floor sweep and nozzle fitting from Air Handling Systems Manufacturers Service Co.

Illus. 7-9. A flexible metal hose from Air Handling Systems Manufacturers Service Co.

grounding wire. Flexible hose is available in many different materials, including metal, cloth and plastic (Illus. 7-9). Illus. 7-10 shows a 4-inch hose with several reducers and a 1¼-inch vacuum hose. The wire-hose connector from Wilke Machinery Co. shown in Illus. 7-10 is excellent for securing the corrugated shape of a collector hose to a fitting.

Special accessories for stationary machines which improve dust pickup are also available. While collecting dust below the saw blade is important, there is also a lot of air dust that comes from the exposed part of the saw blade. Biesemeyer Co. has an extension arm stand that suspends a blade guard and collector hose directly over the saw blade (Illus. 7-11).

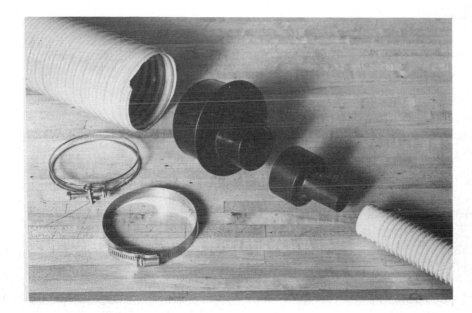

Illus. 7-10. A 4-inch flexible hose with adapters and a 1¼-inch vacuum hose. The wire clamp is designed to secure the corrugated-shaped hose to metal fittings.

Illus. 7-11. A Delta Unisaw and a Biesemeyer guard and dust hose on an extension arm.

Setting Up the Dust Collector

The simplest way to set up a collector is to move it to whichever machine is being used. This might be satisfactory for spacious shops or smaller shops with machines that are operated infrequently. In a smaller shop, however, as the floor becomes congested with tools and lumber, the movable collector is not so easy to move. And if you need to go back and forth frequently between several machines, it becomes a chore to move the collector back and forth.

Another way to set up the collector is to centrally locate it to all machines and use a single flexible hose. This is fairly straightforward in that the hose is connected to whichever machine is being used. Using one length of hose is probably the least expensive system. The disadvantage of this approach is that you will have to move the hose around the shop. The hose will be constantly underfoot, and can be damaged from sharp or heavy objects as it is moved about.

The most efficient, although most expensive, way to set up the collector is to route duct and fittings to each of the various machines. This system certainly requires thorough planning before any installation can be started.

Shop layout is a critical part of setting up the system. It's necessary to select a site for the collector and determine the location of the duct. If your shop is well established, then it will be easier to determine the location and length of duct. However, if your shop is still awaiting future machines, you should factor these into the layout plans. The best strategy is to make a scaled drawing of your workshop and locate all the elements of the shop. Don't forget doors and other potential obstacles.

Once the basic layout is established, look at the details of the system. Determine lengths and diameters of the duct pipes, the number and types of elbows needed, whether they will be 45 or 90 degrees, where to locate the branch ducts and how many to use, which type of branch fitting (T or Y) and slide gates to use and/or how many duct-to-machine fittings there will be in the system. All of these factors will directly influence the efficiency of the dust-collector system.

Most manufacturers of dust-collection systems specify duct lengths and diameters which are optimal for the system. For example, the Delta model 50-181 dust collector is designed to handle a duct run of up to 100 feet using duct which measures 4 to 5 inches in diameter. A duct run is the length of duct pipe going directly from each tool to the collector. Several different runs can use parts of the same branch and main ducts. These branches are controlled by installing slide or blast gates which limit or block air flow. There is no limit to the number of branches in a system, as long as each run does not exceed the maximum length and the air flow is limited to one machine at a time. Remember, the total length of the entire duct system isn't the critical factor in duct layout.

As an aid to determining the requirements of a duct system for your shop, you may want to use a special calculator which is available from Manufacturers Service Co. This easy-to-use calculator in the form of a paper slide rule was designed as an aid for sizing round duct systems and can be used to calculate velocity, cubic feet per minute, equivalent resistance, and static pressure.

Dust-Collection Accessories for Stationary Tools

In most workshops it is a common practice to make fittings and connections that fit between the collector hose and machine. Only a limited number of commercial fittings are available because there are so many variations of tools and hoses that it would not be reasonable to make common fittings. The following are illustrations and de-

Illus. 7-12. A close-up of a lathe with a dust-collection fitting and lamp.

scriptions of several innovative fixtures that woodworkers have made to help collect dust and debris.

The metal fitting shown in Illus. 7-12 is placed as close to the lathe as possible in order to collect the fine sanding dust. The white and dark fittings shown in Illus. 7-13 are plastic rain-gutter fittings. A flexible 4-inch dust hose is connected to the round white fitting. This allows the dust collector to be moved and positioned on the drill-press table relative to the piece being drilled.

When the saw is turned on, a pneumatic device opens the blast gate and then closes it when the saw is turned off.

The band saw shown in Illus. 7-17 has a collector pipe neatly tucked against it. There is also a blast gate made of particle board with a Plexiglas slide at shoulder level. When the collector is operating and the slide is closed, the suction pulls the Plexiglas tight against the upper fitting.

Illus. 7-13. A drill press with a dust-collection fitting made of plastic rain-gutter fittings.

The fitting for the jointer shown in Illus. 7-14 is constructed of plywood and has a clear Plexiglas front window and a shop-made blast gate. The window makes it possible for the tool operator to notice if an obstruction occurs. A similar box is fitted to another machine to the right side of the photograph.

The table saw shown in Illus. 7-15 has a similar box with a Plexiglas window for collecting sawdust from the lower part of the saw. A dust hose has been added to the table saw's guard and is suspended clear of any work.

Illus. 7-16 is a view of the ceiling that is part of the blast-gate system for the table saw shown in Illus. 7-15.

Illus. 7-14. A plywood dust-collection fitting with a Plexiglas viewing window and a custom-made blast gate. The plastic irrigation pipe is grounded with a wire inside the pipe.

Illus. 7-15. A SCMI table saw with a large sliding table. The saw guard is fitted with a dust-collection hose.

Illus. 7-16. A blast gate mounted near a ceiling. It has a pneumatic device that opens and closes it.

The device shown in Illus. 7-18 and 7-19 was designed to remove debris from the planer before it travels to the main collector. Debris enters the Plexiglas-fronted box at the top left side and is diverted downwards via a baffle. Fine dust is pulled upwards into the main duct pipe. There is a gate at the bottom of the funnel in which to empty the box. The wheel in the lower center area operates a stirring device that keeps the debris from clogging the funnel. On the right side of the box is a lever which operates the blast gate slide. By using this device, it is possible to recycle the larger debris from the planer.

The Inca jointer/planer shown in Illus. 7-20–7-22 is

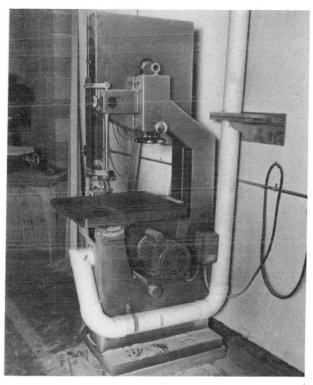

Illus. 7-17. This PVC pipe is customized to the shape of the large band saw.

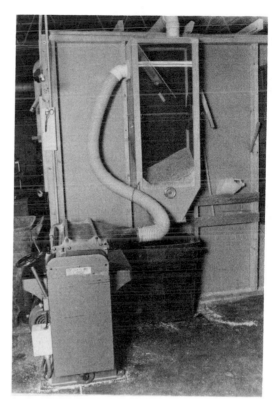

Illus. 7-18. This box is designed to remove planer debris before it passes to the main collector.

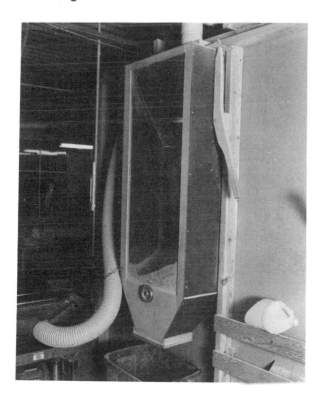

Illus. 7-19. This box has a lever built into its right side which operates the blast-gate slide.

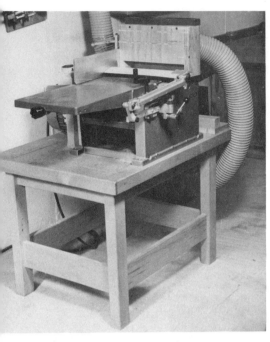

Illus. 7-20 (above left). This dust-collection fitting is attached to an Inca jointer/planer for planing work. **Illus. 7-21 (above right).** A close-up of the fitting for the Inca jointer/planer.

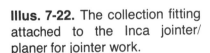

Illus. 7-22. The collection fitting attached to the Inca jointer/planer for jointer work.

designed so that the out-feed table is removed for the planer operation. However, this is awkward if you go back and forth between jointing and planing operations. In order to use either the jointer or the planer without having to do anything with the table, you cannot use the standard collector fitting. Instead, you must make a special collector fitting in the shop. This dust-collector system consists of a wooden box that can be used for either jointer or planer operation. When you are planing, the box sits in front of the cutterhead and is secured by a tab

which fits over the fence. The cutterhead guard is used low over the cutterhead and helps to deflect debris into the collecting slot. When you are jointing, you have to turn the box over so that the collecting slot is at the top and the box is slid into place. A block clamped to the wooden table provides support and restraint to the collector box. Note that when the box is not in place, the other side of the planer has a board which seals off the cavity where dust accumulates.

Space is always at a premium in the small shop. In the

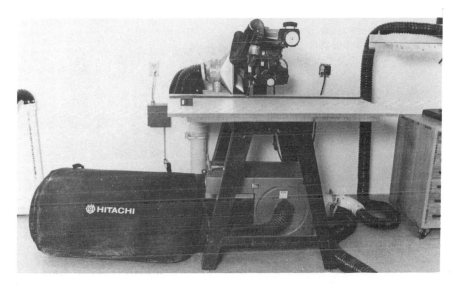

Illus. 7-23. In this small shop, the radial arm saw and dust collector share the same floor space.

shop shown in Illus. 7-23 the dust collector is stored under the radial arm saw. When the collector is not in use, the filter bag is folded close to the legs of the saw.

The "black box" shown in Illus. 7-24 is actually the control for the dust collector. The small device which sits atop the black box is an electric garage door opener, and the black box contains the electrical controls for the opener. The owner had an electrician replace the existing electrical relay with a heavy-duty one to handle the increased power requirements of the dust collector. The small "dust-collector starter" is kept in a shop apron pocket so that the user can activate the dust collector from anywhere in the shop; this eliminates the need to walk back and forth to operate the collector.

Dust-Collection Accessories for Portable Tools

Stationary machines are not the only producers of dust in the shop. Sanders, routers, and joinery machines produce volumes of dust, and, unlike the stationary tools, they fling dust and chips over a very wide area. Even a small finish sander is capable of producing dust everywhere.

For far too long, it seemed that tool manufacturers chose to ignore dust collection. Recently, several companies have made efforts to solve the problem of dust collection. One of the better new products is the hose, dust hood, and dust collector sanding pads that Porter Cable has created for its Random Orbit sander (Illus. 7-25). The hood fits over the disc so that it is close to the work surface, but doesn't interfere with sanding. There are six holes in the sanding discs that go through it, and the sandpaper discs have matching holes (Illus. 7-26.)

Illus. 7-24. This electric garage door opener is modified so that it can be used to switch on the dust collector when the remote control device is activated.

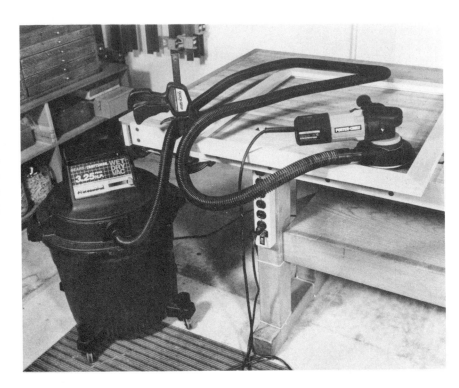

Illus. 7-25. This Porter Cable Random Orbit sander with accessory dust shield and hose is connected to a Sears shop vacuum.

Illus. 7-26. A Porter Cable sander with accessory dust shield and hose. The standard sanding disc pad is at the center of the frame; to the left is a sanding pad with holes. The holes match the sanding discs and dust is pulled through the holes into the vacuum.

Dust is drawn up through the discs and around the edge of the hood. When this dust-collection system is used, dust is no longer a problem when you are sanding.

Makita has also designed a finish sander that has a dust-collection system. This system allows you to hook a shop vacuum directly to the sander. Makita also offers a small bench vacuum that can be used with the sander (Illus. 7-27).

There are many sanders, mitre saws, and other porta-ble tools that come with an attached dust bag. Some companies are now designing their tools so that a shop vacuum hose can be directly attached to the tool. These include Lamello's biscuit joiner, Dremel's model 1695 scroll saw (Illus. 7-28 and 7-29), and the Sears' finish and belt sanders. Note in Illus. 7-30 the use of an accessory fitting which allows a vacuum hose to be fitted to both of the sanding tools.

Hitachi offers a clear-plastic collector fitting (Illus.

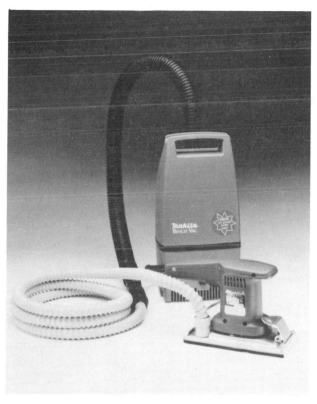

Illus. 7-27. A Makita finishing sander and bench vacuum.

Illus. 7-28. The Dremel model 1695 scroll saw has a built-in fitting for a dust-collection hose.

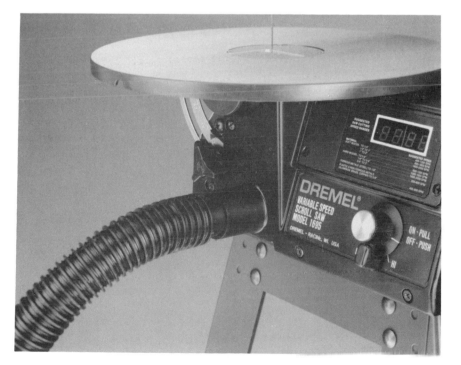

Illus. 7-29. A close-up view of how the dust hose fits the Dremel scroll saw.

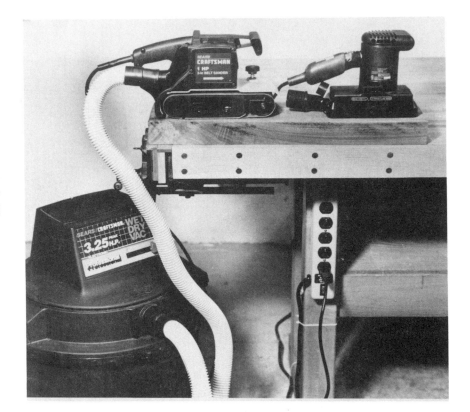

Illus. 7-30. The accessory fitting permits a dust-collection hose to fit the Sears belt and finishing sanders.

Illus. 7-31. A Hitachi accessory dust-hose fitting for a router.

Illus. 7-32. A Hitachi router with a dust hose fitting with clearance over the work area.

7-31) for most of its routers, and a vacuum hose adapter for its compound mitre saw. In Illus. 7-32, note that the Hitachi router, fitting, and hose are clear of the L-shaped edge guide and clamp.

Special Dust-Collection Accessories

The Automater from R. F. St. Louis Associates is a device that automatically turns on the collector when the power tool is switched on. It plugs into the AC outlet, and has two AC outlets of its own. The control outlet is for the power tool; the switching outlet is for the dust collector. When the tool is switched on, the dust collector is automatically switched on. When the tool is switched off, the dust collector is automatically switched off. Several versions of the Automater are available. The Automater is also very useful when you are using smaller tools, such as the plate jointer, that are switched on and off for quick, successive cuts. Simply connect the power tool and shop vacuum to the Automater.

Lathe turners have popularized a unique product that provides clean air while they are turning. The debris from turning usually scatters in such a way that it is difficult for collectors to catch all of the shavings and dust. The Airstream Helmet (Illus. 7-33) is a 1.9-pound helmet which provides a clear face visor, helmet, filter and battery pack. Contaminated air is drawn into the filters at the rear of the helmet and clean air is delivered down across the face and then exhausted below the chin. This provides the operator with mobility, positive pressure behind the face shield, and a positive flow of purified air. The

Airstream Helmet can be worn over goggles, glasses, beards, and long hair.

Illus. 7-33. The Airstream Helmet with built-in fan and filter system.

CHAPTER EIGHT

Creating a Mobile Workshop

One problem most woodworkers face is how to best utilize the workshop so that the several heavy machines in it can be moved around, should the need arise. There are three solutions to this problem: Work in a very spacious shop, replace multiple stand-alone machines with a single combination machine, or make the machines portable. While having a large shop sounds great, it's not a reality for most woodworkers. Combination machines can be extremely useful, if they contain the right combination of functions and are ruggedly built. But the simplest solution is to put the machines on wheels and move them as necessary.

Mobile Bases

A mobile machine should be one that can be easily and quickly moved by anyone in the shop. Mobile bases have been around as machine accessories for a long time, and can be extremely useful. Machines that are used only occasionally or are difficult to move can be used and then easily rolled to an out-of-the-way location if they have mobile bases. Machines that are frequently used could be quickly moved for cleaning or for minor positional adjustments. And machines such as a radial arm saw that are easily knocked out of alignment when normally moved could be moved on a mobile base and still remain in alignment.

Some mobile bases are versions of shop-made devices that are essentially drop-down wheels that can be attached to one side of a machine. These types of base are not very good because the woodworker has to raise its opposite side arms with his back, and legs. If the machine weighs several hundred pounds, this can be a tremendous physical strain on the individual and a strain on the machine parts that are used as handles (the table edge or table rails). After the machine is lifted into position on the "base," it can be moved somewhat like on a wheelbarrow.

The modern mobile base is streamlined, has a low profile, and is not as difficult to use. Because the bases fit reasonably close to the machine, they pose no obstruction to feet or other moving things in the shop. The mobile bases made by Delta Corp. and HTC Products Co. raise the machine approximately ¾ inch from the floor, and the machine sets within the framework of the base. The HTC mobile base (Illus. 8-1) has threaded securing knobs that are used to immobilize or free the front two wheels. Just loosen the knobs to move the machine, and then re-tighten them to make the machine stationary again. The Delta Co. mobile base (Illus. 8-2) is controlled by a lever-activated wheel. By lifting or lowering the lever, you can engage or disengage the wheels. Both the Delta and HTC mobile bases have pivoting wheels that allow the machine to be easily moved in any direction. Illus. 8-2 shows the quick connectors that are used to connect the sander to the dust collector. This is essential if machines are to be moved about the workshop.

HTC bases are available for most models of different manufacturers' machines (Illus. 8-3), and the company routinely makes custom bases for older machines or ones with unusually shaped bases. Delta's mobile bases are specifically made to match the pattern of its product (Illus. 3-4). However, if you measure the base of a machine not manufactured by Delta, you might find that it matches the size of a Delta mobile base.

These mobile bases are very helpful because machines

Illus. 8-1 (above left). An HTC Products mobile base frame. Note the pilot wheel and wheel housing on the side of the frame, which has a locking knob to stop the base from moving. **Illus. 8-2 (above right).** The Delta mobile base. The lever is moved to raise or lower the pilot wheel. The Delta base also has rubber feet, as well as wheels. Note the quick connector fitting on the dust collection hoses.

Illus. 8-3. An HTC Products mobile base being used with an Inca table saw.

Illus. 8-4. A Delta Unisaw and extension table being used with a matching Delta mobile base.

Illus. 8-5. Mobile bases make it easy to store machinery when it is not being used.

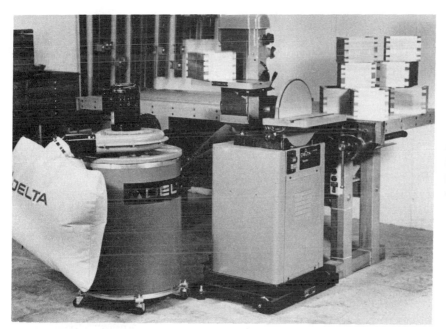

Illus. 8-6. The Delta floor-model sander and dust collector have been rolled next to the workbench to make it easier to work with numerous pieces.

Illus. 8-7. A custom-made mobile cabinet with lockable wheels that is being used with a small band saw

that are not used all the time, such as a finishing sander, can be placed against a wall when they are not needed (Illus. 8-5), and then rolled next to the workbench for use. This is a convenient arrangement, because it eliminates the need for another permanent table in the shop to hold objects as they are being sanded (Illus. 8-6).

A shop-made mobile base that is effective is shown in Illus. 8-7. The band saw is lightweight and lends itself to a roller cabinet. The cabinet has lockable wheels and enough storage for band-saw accessories as well as miscellaneous items. This design would work for a variety of bench tools, including tabletop drill presses, portable planers, and mitre saws.

Roller Tables

HTC Products has several versatile roller tables. Shown in Illus. 8-8 and 8-9 are two roller tables that have been built into the mobile base that make handling lumber safer and easier. These roller tables are available in several sizes as measured by the length of the table. A model with five rollers that is ideal for the small shop is shown in Illus. 8-10. The roller table easily supports a $1\frac{1}{2} \times 7 \times 96$-inch board, so it can be resawn and controlled by one person (Illus. 8-11). Another variation of the roller table is shown in Illus. 8-12 and 8-13. The roller table is attached to the out-feed side of the table saw and is pivoted to a horizontal position, flush with the tabletop, when needed. It can then be pivoted to a vertical position against the back of the saw for storage.

Illus. 8-8 (above left). An HTC Products mobile stand with single rollers on either side of a small planer. **Illus. 8-9 (above right).** An HTC Products mobile stand with long roller tables that fold out of the way when not in use.

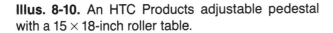

Illus. 8-10. An HTC Products adjustable pedestal with a 15 × 18-inch roller table.

Illus. 8-11. This roller stand is supporting a long board on a band saw.

Illus. 8-12. This roller table is attached to the out-feed side of the table saw.

Illus. 8-13. The roller table is now folded in against the table saw.

Brett Guard

Illus. 8-14 shows a mobile base, an out-feed roller table, and a Brett guard positioned over a sheet of plywood. The guard is a clear shield and functions as both a safety and hold-down device. It is wide enough to permit ripping, crosscutting, and bevel-cutting. The shield comes with a splitter (riving knife), an adjustable anti-kickback device, an auxiliary stop button, and a lock switch for controlling access to the machine (Illus. 8-15). The Brett guard covers the blade and cutting action when bevel cuts are made, and can be locked to prevent unauthorized usage of the saw. While the Brett guard is used in many schools, its features can also be useful in the home workshop.

Lumber Cart

Lifting and moving lumber or plywood has always been a strenuous task, especially for one person. For the one-person shop, a single sheet of plywood is cumbersome to position for sawing. Also, wood material such as a single sheet of medium density fibreboard (MDF) can weigh as much as 100 pounds. In larger shops, it is not uncommon to find extension tables mounted to the side and rear of table saws to accommodate larger workpieces (Illus. 8-16).

The Shopcart offers an improved method for handling materials for both small and large workshops. It features a pivoting and tilting carriage which measures 30 inches wide by 48 inches long. Vertical height is adjusted with a foot-operated hydraulic jack that can elevate the carriage from 27 to 35 inches (Illus. 8-17).

The Shopcart is conservatively rated for a load of 600 pounds. This means that as many as ten sheets of ¾-inch-thick plywood can be moved in one load. To use the Shopcart, place the carriage in a horizontal position, step

Illus. 8-14. A Brett guard is mounted on the Delta Unisaw.

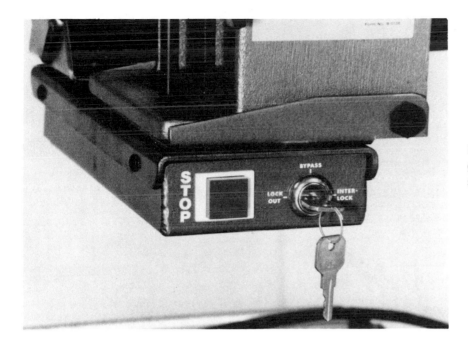

Illus. 8-15. A close-up of the Brett guard stop button and lock switch.

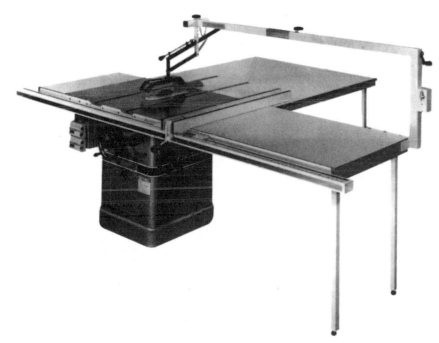

Illus. 8-16. This table saw has side and rear extension tables. The Biesemeyer guard is attached to a long support arm.

on the floor lock to keep the cart from moving, and slide the material onto the cart.

The Shopcart can also be used as both an in-feed and out-feed table. Illus. 8-18 shows the Shopcart in use as an in-feed table for the table saw. In Illus. 8-19, the Shopcart is being used as an out-feed table for a jointer to stabilize long workpieces. The height of the Shopcart is easily

adjusted to different table heights with its hydraulic jack.

If work material has to be moved through a narrow door opening or to a panel saw, the carriage can be pivoted to a vertical position. The pivot point is slightly off-center, which makes it easy to rotate the carriage even with a full load in place.

Illus. 8-17 (above left). The Shopcart is a heavy-duty cart with a hydraulic-controlled carriage which can be positioned both horizontally or vertically. **Illus. 8-18 (above right).** The Shopcart used as an auxiliary in-feed table. The stack of plywood is hydraulically adjusted so that the top sheet is always at the same height as the table saw.

Illus. 8-19. The Shopcart used as an auxiliary out-feed table at the jointer.

CHAPTER NINE

Air Compressors and Air Tools

At one time only automobile painters, tire and muffler stores, and a few commercial woodworkers routinely used air tools. Today, not only are air compressors and air tools used in the workshop, but product selection is greater than ever.

Sanding, grinding, drilling, carving, nailing, clamping, blowing dust, and painting are the principal applications of air compressors and air tools for the woodworker.

Air Nailers

When I first purchased a compressor, I used it for blowing dust off workpieces and machines and for cleaning the shop. Sometime later while I was remodelling our house, I injured a shoulder muscle and found it impossible to swing a hammer without experiencing a lot of pain. Since it was not feasible for me to rest for a week or two, I purchased two nail guns similar to the ones shown in Illus. 8-1. One was a small gun which used headless ⅝ to 1-inch-long pins or brads. The other was also a finish nailer which used headless 1½ to 2½-inch-long nails. With these nail guns, I could drive nails all day long. Not only that, it was now easier to hold a brace or moulding in an overhead position and nail it in place.

There was another advantage. Normally, one drills a

Illus. 9-1. A Bostich brad nailer and a Senco nailer. The Bostich nailer uses ⅝-, ¾-, and 1-inch headless brads. The Senco nailer uses 1½-, 2-, and 2½-inch headless finishing nails. Note that the nails are in strips.

pilot hole before hammering a nail into hardwoods. This allows the nail to actually penetrate the hardwood, and minimizes the likelihood of splitting the wood. But the nail gun literally "shoots" the nail into the wood, and the chance of splitting is almost completely eliminated in both hard and soft woods. Also, an air nailer is designed to sink the nail head below the surface of the wood, thus eliminating the chance of damaging the wood surface as can occur when using a hammer and nailset.

After the remodelling was finished, I was not sure whether I would find other uses for the nail guns. However, I have found that the smaller nail gun is ideal for making workshop jigs and fixtures, and the larger one for making shipping crates and plywood cabinets. Both nail guns are now part of my hammer collection!

Other Air Tools

Other air tools that I now use frequently include spray guns, a cut-off tool for cutting metal rods and parts, a grinder for shaping metal pieces, and a rotary sander and straight-line sanders for quick stock removal and shaping (Illus. 9-2 and 9-3). The ratchet wrench shown in Illus. 9-3 was used to tighten the 50 or more square-drive screws in a futon bed frame. I use the 60-pound capacity sandblaster shown in Illus. 9-4 to remove rust and paint from metal outdoor tabletops and wooden window shutters, and the small abrasive gun with a 4-ounce-capacity jar to etch designs on glass and to remove light rust and corrosion from tools. The air compressor shown in Illus. 9-4 is also used to power air clamps and presses, staplers, drills, impact wrenches, hammers, and saws.

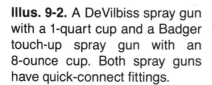

Illus. 9-2. A DeVilbiss spray gun with a 1-quart cup and a Badger touch-up spray gun with an 8-ounce cup. Both spray guns have quick-connect fittings.

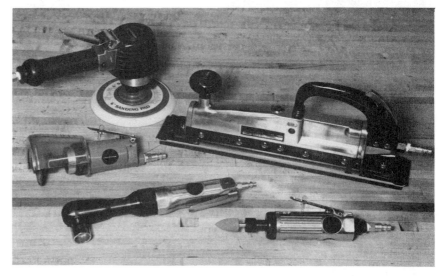

Illus. 9-3. Sears air tools. Clockwise, starting from top left, are a rotary sander, straight-line sander, die grinder, ratchet wrench, and cutter. All tools have quick-connect fittings.

Illus. 9-4. A Sears 60-pound capacity sandblaster and a Badger abrasive gun with 4-ounce-capacity jar.

Illus. 9-5. This table is set up for airbrush work. The airbrush rests in a holder at the right side of the table and is connected to a pressure regulator. Cardboard is used to reduce over-spray.

Illus. 9-6. A close-up view of the air-brush, jars, cup, head assembly piece, and holder.

Using an airbrush is surprisingly easy. Set up a table for the airbrush in a clean part of the shop, install the air regulator, and attach the airbrush hose. Using the airbrush is similar to using an aerosol can, except that there is more control, less waste, and the material is sprayed more evenly. Many woodworkers use airbrushes to paint stencil patterns on various pieces of furniture. Illus. 9-6 shows a model automobile that is being painted by my children.

Air Clamps and Presses

Air clamps are used to hold a piece of wood for a particular operation (Illus. 9-7 and 9-8). Generally, air clamps are held in a frame or are attached to a secured post. The air clamp is operated by either a foot pedal or a lever on a regulator device. It's ideal as a securing device. Once an air clamp is set to a specific wood thickness, it is ideal for repetitive or production-type work.

Air, or vacuum, presses are ideal for veneering applications. Basically, the system consists of a vacuum pump, a vinyl or polyurethane bag, and a grooved-surface sheet of particle board (Illus. 9-9 and 9-10). The workpiece and veneer are prepared in the usual manner and then slid into the pliable press bag over the top of the grooved board. The bag is sealed and the pump is activated. Pressure is created within the bag, and the bag shapes itself over the workpiece and veneer. Pressure is applied evenly over the workpiece, there is no slippage between the layers, and glue is sucked into the porous wood cells. The vacuum press works on flat, curved or shaped workpieces.

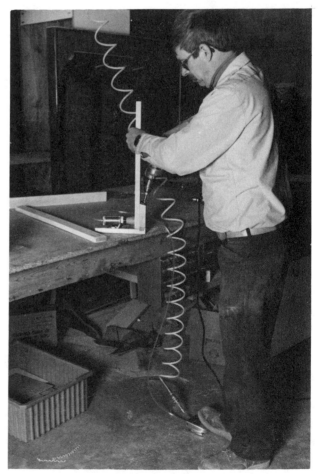

Illus. 9-7. A Kreg Jig with an air clamp. Note the coiled air hose and foot switch.

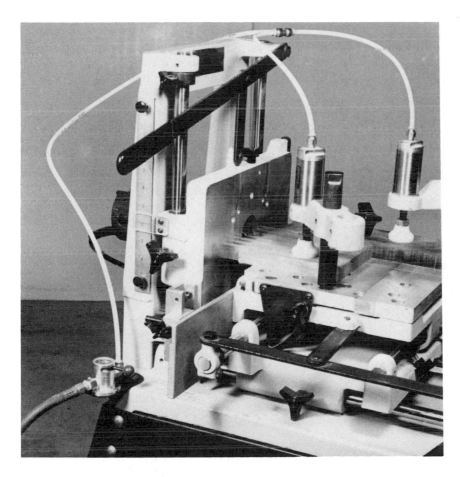

Illus. 9-8. This Multi-Router join-ery machine is being used with air clamps and an on/off regu-lator.

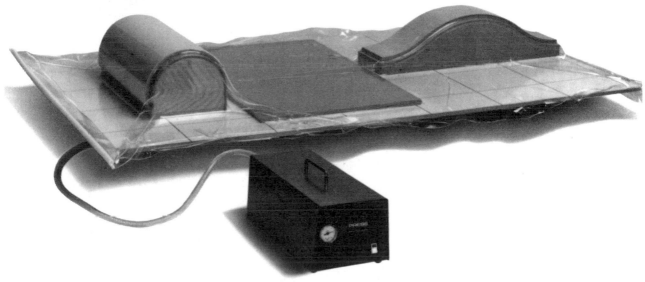

Illus. 9-9. This vacuum press from Vacuum Pressing Systems consists of a pump and plastic bag with an internal board. The system is ideal for clamping veneers on any type of surface, no matter what shape it is.

Illus. 9-10. The slotted board inside the bag of a vacuum press system. The slots allow air to be pumped out and the bag to smoothly fit over the workpiece.

The Vacupress, from Vacuum Pressing Systems, Inc., is a ¼-horsepower oil-less rotary vane vacuum pump with thermal overload protection. It uses 5 cfm and reaches a maximum vacuum of 1,774 pounds per square inch in about 2 minutes. While these units are expensive, the alternative of building clamping frames especially for veneering and buying special-purpose clamps is also expensive, especially if the veneering project is on a curved or shaped workpiece.

The vacuum press can also be used as a clamp. The Woodhaven vacuum clamp shown in Illus. 9-11 and 9-12 is driven by an air compressor requiring 2 cfm and 40 to 80 psi. The workpiece is held by vacuum against a template which offers fast, obstruction-free clamping for single or many pieces. The template in Illus. 9-11 is holding a workpiece that is being shaped on a router table with a ball-bearing flush trimming bit. The template of any vacuum clamp system should have about 100 square inches of surface area, which yields approximately 900 pounds of holding force. It is made of any nonporous material, including medium-density fibreboard, die board, and acrylic.

The Edge Finisher Corp. vacuum clamp shown in Illus. 9-13 and 9-14 is driven by a 110-volt electric pump motor

Illus. 9-11. A vacuum clamp system from Woodhaven. The clamp is securing a workpiece for work on a router table.

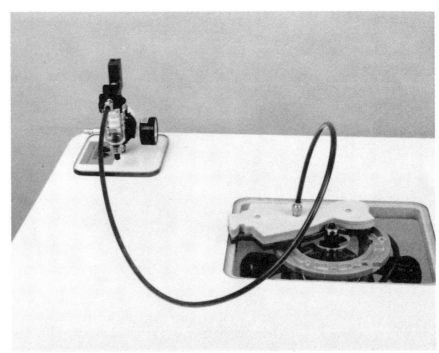

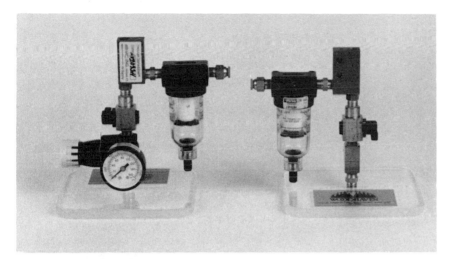

Illus. 9-12. A close-up of the Woodhaven vacuum clamp.

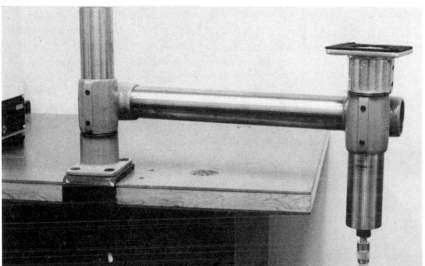

Illus. 9-13. A vacuum clamp from Edge Finisher Corp.

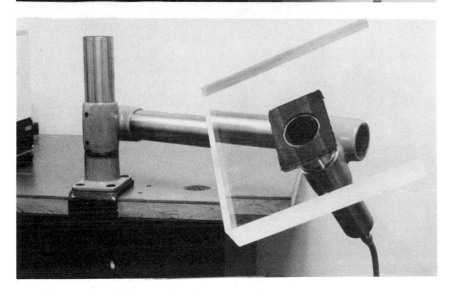

Illus. 9-14. The vacuum clamp is holding a large block of Plexiglas.

which sits on the floor. The vacuum clamp is positioned on an arm assembly which is mounted on the bench. The workpieces require a surface area of approximately 100 square inches for maximum clamping. This system also offers an obstruction-free work area and is ideal for holding workpieces for routing, edge-banding, carving, lettering, and other work that is best done in an upright (at the workbench) position.

Air Compressors

The air compressor is the power source that makes all the tools described in this chapter useful (Illus. 9-15). Yet all too often the air compressor is operated with disregard for its features, adjustments and required maintenance. There are many different types of standard air compressors: those with large or small tank capacities, portable or stationary compressors, and electric- or gasoline-powered compressors. These air compressors have a wide range of capacities for air delivery.

There are two basic types of compressors: those with air tanks and those that do not have air tanks. Those without air tanks are less expensive than the compressors with air tanks, and are designed primarily for blowing air and inflating tubes and tires. This type is usually not designed to drive air tools, except for specialized applications such as airbrush painting. Compressors with air tanks are more powerful and, depending upon the model, will operate any air tool or accessory.

Air-Compressor Components

Physical features of compressors with air tanks typically include a shut-off valve, check valve, pressure-release valve, pressure switch, safety valve, regulator, drain valve, outlet pressure gauge and tank pressure gauge. Air delivery to the tool is measured in pounds per square inch (psi) and standard cubic feet per minute (scfm).

The *shut-off valve* is a knob or lever which releases air from the tank. The *check valve* opens to allow air into the tank when the compressor is running. When the compressor reaches the "cut-out" pressure, the check valve closes to maintain the air-pressure level inside the tank.

The *pressure-release valve* is associated with the pressure switch, and either automatically releases compressed air from the compressor head and outlet tube when the air compressor reaches its "cut-out" pressure or is shut off. If the air were not released, the motor would try to start, but wouldn't be able to. The pressure-release valve allows the motor to restart freely. When the motor stops running, air can be heard escaping from the valve for a few seconds. No air should be heard leaking when the motor is running.

The *pressure switch* automatically starts the motor when the pressure in the air tank drops below the factory-set "cut-in" pressure. It also stops the motor when the pressure in the air tank reaches the factory-set "cut-out" pressure.

The *safety valve* prevents the pressure from building up too high within the air tank and is designed to open at a

Illus. 9-15. A Sears 3½-horsepower air compressor. It features a 15-gallon tank, and runs at 8.5 scfm at 40 psi and 7.0 scfm at 90 psi.

factory-set pressure. This is added protection in the event the pressure switch fails to shut off the compressor at its "cut-out" pressure setting.

The *regulator* controls the air pressure coming from the air tank. By turning the regulator knob, you can increase or decrease the air pressure that is released.

The *drain valve* is located on the bottom of the tank. Occasionally the air inside the tank should be released, and the drain valve opened to drain off any water that has condensed within the tank. This prevents the tank from rusting on the inside.

The *outlet pressure gauge* indicates the air pressure available at the outlet side of the regulator. This pressure is controlled by the regulator and is always less than or equal to the tank pressure. The *tank pressure gauge* indicates the reserve air pressure in the tank.

Some compressors are permanently lubricated, and others need to have oil periodically added to the crankcase. A special oil is usually available from stores that sell air compressors.

The three major factors which should be considered when selecting an air compressor are horsepower (hp), standard cubic feet per minute (scfm), and tank capacity. A good range of horsepower for the workshop is from 1 to 5 horsepower. Although there are air compressors with greater horsepower, these tend to be more expensive, as well as larger and heavier.

When you are deciding upon horsepower, consider the kind of work you plan to do. If you plan to use the air compressor for brief periods of time or simply to blow dust out of the workshop, then an air compressor with a lower horsepower rating will probably be adequate. If, however, you plan to use air tools continuously in a heavy-duty fashion, then choose an air compressor with a higher horsepower rating.

Standard cubic feet per minute (scfm) is related to horsepower, and is a standard measurement nomenclature that is used throughout the industry. It is a measure of air delivery from the air compressor to the air tool. For example, a compressor with a higher rated scfm forces more air through the air hose. Air compressors with more horsepower will have more scfm than those with less horsepower, and are better able to produce the air pressure necessary to continuously operate air tools.

Most workshop compressors are rated at approximately 90 to 120 psi (pounds per square inch). Unlike scfm, the psi of a compressor can be adjusted via the regulator for different tools and job applications. Air compressors with a low psi rating are typically intended for specific applications such as air-brushing. Air compressors with a high psi rating can be used to spray a heavier body of paint, and can more efficiently operate air tools.

The best way to select an air compressor is to first list the air tools that you plan to use and note their required scfm's, and then choose an air compressor to match these requirements. People often buy an air compressor first (perhaps because of a great sale price) and then find out that the air tools they bought afterwards require more air delivery than the compressor can supply. Consequently, no matter how frequently the air compressor is running, it cannot produce enough scfm to make the tool work.

Air-Tool Requirements

Chart 9-1 is representative of various air-tool requirements.

A Sampling of Air Compressors

Chart 9-2 lists the specifications of nine different compressors. Other models are available, but these compressors were selected as being representative.

Setting Up the Air-Compressor System

There are three ways to set up an air-compressor system: Use it as a portable tool, and roll from one work location to the next; use it as a stationary tool, and keep it in a permanent, fixed location; or set it up to be used as either a portable or stationary tool.

Most compressors are small enough to be portable. Some can be picked up and carried, while others have wheels and a tote handle. One popular construction-site compressor is referred to as the "wheelbarrow," for the obvious reason that the compressor has a single wheel in the front and two handles sticking out from the rear.

There are certain things to be aware of when using the compressor, either in the backyard or at a house construction site. If at all possible, keep the air compressor close to an AC outlet and avoid the use of extension cords. Extension cords lead to voltage drops which can cause the motor to overheat or fail to start. If you must use an extension cord, use one with a three-blade grounding plug that has a 12-gauge (AWG) or larger cord. Also, make sure that the extension cord is in good condition. The longer the extension cord, the greater the voltage drop, so use one that is as short as possible. Also, try to have a dedicated circuit of at least 15 amps. If this is not possible, keep the circuit free of other electrical demands.

Tool	scfm	hp (compressor)	psi
Airbrush	1–2	$\frac{1}{20}$–$\frac{1}{2}$	15–50
Spray guns	$1\frac{7}{10}$–$8\frac{1}{2}$	$\frac{3}{4}$–3	30–40
Drill	3–4	1	90–100
Rotary sander	4–5	1	90–100
Straight-line sander	8	2	90–100
Finish sander	4	2	90–100
Random orbital sander	4	2	90–100
Impact hammer	3–4	1	90–100
Die grinder	5–6	1	90–100
Cut-off tool	4	1	90–100
Impact wrench	4–8	1	90–100
Ratchet wrench	$2\frac{1}{2}$–4	1	90–100
Sandblaster	$4\frac{1}{2}$	1	40
Nailers and staplers	2–9	$\frac{1}{2}$–1	70–120

Chart 9-1.

HP	Tank Capacity (gallons)	SCFM	Product
$\frac{1}{12}$	no tank	0.8 @ 20 psi	Whirlwind II, model 80-2
$\frac{1}{2}$	$1\frac{1}{2}$	2.3 @ 30 psi/$1\frac{8}{10}$ @ 50 psi	Hurricane, model 180-4
$\frac{3}{4}$	3	2.7 @ 40 psi/2 @ 90 psi	Campbell Hausfeld, model MT-5004
1	$4\frac{1}{2}$	2.95 @ 59 psi/2.55 @ 100 psi	Thomas Turbo Pancake, model T50-234
$1\frac{1}{2}$	8	4.5 @ 40 psi/3.2 @ 90 psi	Sears Craftsman, model 15431
2	4(x 2 tanks)	7.1 @ 40 psi/6.2 @ 90 psi	Industrial Air, model 20TE8P
2	8	9.8 @ 40 psi/7.9 @ 90 psi	Emglo, model K2A-8P
$3\frac{1}{2}$	15	8.5 @ 40 psi/6.8 @ 90 psi	Sears Craftsman, model 15353
5	30	12 @ 40 psi/10 @ 90 psi	Sears Craftsman, model 17695

Chart 9-2.

Air Hose

Instead of using extension cords, consider using additional air hoses. Air hoses are available in either 25- or 50-foot prepared lengths, and some hardware stores can prepare hoses of any length. Hoses are generally available, either straight or coiled, in $\frac{1}{4}$-, $\frac{5}{16}$-, and $\frac{3}{8}$-inch diameters. Straight hoses that are $\frac{3}{8}$ inch in diameter and 25 feet long are good for general work. This type of hose is durable enough for shop work, and delivers the correct volume of air for most air tools. Also, if work has to be done some distance from the hose, several hoses 25 feet long can be connected to the principal hose. Also helpful are coiled hoses suspended from the ceiling near the workbench. These hoses are convenient, yet are out of the way when not needed. In Illus. 9-16, the air hose is secured to the compressor handle with electrical tie-wraps so that there will be no unnecessary strain on the hose coupler and fitting. An air hose often develops an air leak because the hose fitting has been damaged as a result of the air hose being repeatedly pulled sideways. The plastic tie-wraps were designed to secure electrical wiring, but they can be used in many other applications. (The tie-wraps in Illus. 9-16 were deliberately left long so that they would be visible in the photograph; usually, they can be trimmed with wire-cutting pliers.)

An alternative to using hoses is to install metal pipe from the compressor and along the shop walls. Pipe length and diameter are important factors; the greater the length of the pipe, the greater the loss of air pressure. Main lines should be sized to account for future requirements as well as the effects of pipe aging. As the inside of the pipes age, they can rust and corrode, and this internal roughness can cause additional pressure loss.

Illus. 9-16. Electrical tie-wraps used as strain reliefs. The air hose is secured to the handle so that the hose fitting is not accidentally damaged if pulled at an awkward angle. The tie-wraps can be trimmed shorter.

When installing a pipe-system slope, the main line down as it extends away from the compressor should be about ⅛ to ¼ inch per foot, or about 1 inch per 10 feet of length. Air flow and gravity will move moisture and other particles to the filter. To create branches off the main pipe, install T-fittings with shut-off valves and attach hoses.

Regulating Air Pressure

The air pressure at the regulator is actually controlled by the entire air system. Any internal roughness within the pipe, elbows, couplers, filters, and other fittings will restrict air flow. To get an indicator of air flow, measure the pressure at the end of the outlet with a T-pressure gauge positioned between the air tool and outlet. Using a nail gun as a test, simply activate the tool to simulate

normal operating speed. For example, if you have set the regulator so that the tool receives 100 psi, the air flow is good if after three to five triggerings the T-gauge shows 100 to 97 psi. If, however, the pressure drops to 85 psi, then there is a greater drop in pressure than is normal. This may require you to check the pressure readings on both sides of the various line components to find the problem.

Selecting the location for the compressor in the workshop is crucial. Locate the compressor so that it does not become covered with dust. Compressors have filters on their air intakes, but the filter can become clogged with too much dust. Compressors tend to be noisy when their motors are operating, so you may want to position yours slightly away from the workbench or general work area. The disadvantage of placing the compressor away from the work area is the distance and placement of the air delivery system. If you use hoses, be careful of cluttering the floor with loops of hose. If you install pipe along the wall, carefully plan the pipe route so that it is clear of wall cabinets and other tools, yet at the same time offers convenient drop-line locations.

Preparing Air for Air Tools

No matter whether you use hose or pipe as a delivery system, the compressed air needs to be prepared for the air tools. The most common preparation is removing condensation from the air delivery system. Condensation is the result of the compressor drawing moist air into the tank. This occurs in most areas of the country, and can be especially noticeable in basements and open garages. Another way for moist air to reach the air tool is through the process of air pressurization. Air is warmed as it is pressurized in the tank due to the operation of the motor pump, and then cools while not being used in the air hoses or lines. This cycle of warming and cooling produces moisture.

Paint spray guns require clean air that is free of moisture and oil. There is nothing more unsatisfactory than spraying a lacquer or varnish and ending up with a mottled and flawed finish. And moisture can cause the metal parts of many air tools to rust and stick. Air tools, like spray guns, work best with moisture-free air.

The common practice of attaching the filter onto the outlet fitting on the air compressor only removes moisture from the tank, and does nothing about removing the moisture in the hose or line. For spray painting, install an in-line filter and regulator as near to the spray gun as possible. If you are using hoses, connect a hose between the compressor and the filter so that the hose is bowed towards the floor between the two. Connect another hose from the regulator side of the filter to the spray gun. Moisture will settle in the bowed section of the hose, and the filter will trap water before it reaches the spray gun. The hose can be periodically disconnected and blown out. And the filter can also be routinely drained and cleaned. Remember, the compressor tank should also be periodically drained.

Another useful accessory is a regulator. This is positioned between a length of hose and the air tank. The tank can be maintained at its normal operating pressure, and the regulator is used to adjust the amount of air pressure at the outlet end. And, if you use long lengths of air hose, there will be some pressure drop at the outlet end. The regulator can be used to compensate or adjust for this drop. Simply squeeze the air tool trigger, and at the same time adjust the regulator to the desired psi.

Illus. 9-17 and 9-18 show one solution for keeping the filter and regulator as close to the work as possible. The filter/regulator (Illus. 9-18) is attached to a board which is mounted to a stud board. This setup can be located anywhere in the shop by simply clamping the top of the stud board to an overhead joist. It can even be moved

Illus. 9-17 (right). Proper conditioning of the air compressor requires the use of a filter and regulator. The filter/regulator is mounted to a board that can be located anywhere in the shop.

Illus. 9-18. A close-up of the filter/regulator.

outside if there is a need for outdoor work. There, the portable stud board can be clamped to a ladder or other solid object.

There are two methods for oiling air tools. The first is to set the compressor, hose, filter, and regulator as described for spray guns. To oil the air tools, simply put drops of pneumatic tool oil directly into the tool. This is certainly the best method if you use both air tools and spray guns, and have only one hose-and-filter system.

The second method consists of installing an oil-fog lubricator between the moisture filter and the air tool. If you use this method, remember that oil will be blown through the hose or line, so it cannot be used for painting.

One other note concerning setup. Hoses can be directly threaded to spray guns and air tools, but quick connectors are much better. Using quick connectors simplifies the process of adding more hoses or changing tools. Quick connectors are composed of two parts: the stud and the coupler. The stud is threaded to the tool or

gun and the coupler is attached to the hose. To use the quick connector, simply slide back the spring-loaded shut-off valve on the coupler, insert the stud into the coupler, and release the spring-loaded slide. Use Teflon tape for all threaded fittings from the compressor to the tools and spray guns.

Finally, it is not wise to buy used or old compressors. It is tempting to buy a compressor at a garage sale or through the classified ads, but it is impossible to know the condition of the inside of the tank. Tanks rust from the inside out. If a tank is properly drained, it can have a reasonable life span. If the tank isn't maintained, it can literally fill up with water and rust quickly. When 120 pounds of air pressure push on the wall of a tank that has thinned from rusting, the potential for problems exists. Absolutely never buy or use a compressor that has "repaired" pin holes in the tank. Air compressors are definitely best and safest when purchased new!

CHAPTER TEN

Spray-Painting Systems

If you were offered a spray-painting system that was easy to use and would reduce your supply costs by 30 to 50 percent, you would certainly consider using it. High-Volume and Low-Pressure (HVLP) systems are becoming popular for these very reasons. They reflect the future direction of United States' policies on atmospheric air quality. The days of unrestricted spray painting are rapidly drawing to a close. There are now rules which govern the types of finishes and how these finishes are applied. These rules will affect traditional spraying methods, and some rules specifically name the HVLP spray as one of the approved systems for applying finishes.

HVLP systems are very efficient systems which produce minimal overspray. Overspray is the cloud of sprayed material that doesn't go on to the workpiece. Instead, the sprayed material lingers in the air or is vented to the outside by a fan. Less overspray means that less finishing material is released into the atmosphere. The South Coast Air Quality Management district (Los Angeles, California) estimates that conventional compressed-air spray systems have approximately a 25-percent transfer efficiency, airless spray systems have approximately a 40-percent efficiency, and the HVLP spray systems have about an 80- to 90-percent transfer efficiency.

Clearly, the benefits of the HVLP system for the workshop are less overspray, less spray bounceback, and more control of the spray pattern. These features result in a cost savings on materials because less finishing material is wasted, and a cleaner and healthier environment for the operator. Another benefit of HVLP systems is that there is no oil or moisture in the system. Contamination from the oils which are used to lubricate the compressor pump motor or air tools, or moisture caused by condensation of air in the storage tank, can affect the spray finish in air-compressor systems. "Blushing" is one example of the

problems caused by moisture in lacquer as it is applied.

In terms of the final surface finish, HVLP systems perform as well as conventional compressor spray guns. In fact, many commercial painting companies, such as auto body shops, sign makers, appliance shops, and wood finishers, have been using HVLP systems for some time because they produce good finishes.

The HVLP system is considerably different than the standard air-compressor spraying systems. HVLP systems can only be used for spraying finishes and some glues, and cannot be used as a power source for other air tools. HVLP systems don't use a tank system for air management. Instead they generate air directly from either an air-conversion gun/system, or a turbine/impeller system. Also, traditional high-pressure spray guns won't work with the HVLP systems. HVLP systems need a spray gun that is specially designed for the system.

Woodworkers who have invested in traditional air compressors which are used for functions other than spraying don't necessarily need to replace these units. Instead, they can, and often do, use a conversion spray gun that converts the normal high-pressure compressed air produced by an air compressor to the low-pressure air required for the HVLP system. The Accuspray conversion gun (Illus. 10-1) is designed specifically for low-pressure spraying. The moulded composite body has large sweeping air passages to minimize air turbulence and improve atomization of the coating particles. Low-pressure air travels through the gun to the air cap at the same pressure that it enters the gun. If you decide to purchase a conversion gun, be certain to verify that the gun isn't simply a converted high-pressure gun with narrow air passages.

Besides cost, the one significant limitation to conversion guns, especially if you have a low-horsepower air compressor, is that these guns require 6 to 18 scfm,

Illus. 10-1. The Accuspray HVLP conversion spray gun.

The complete HVLP system has a portable turbine/air impeller system, a large-diameter air hose and a HVLP spray gun (Illus. 10-2–10-4). The turbine produces a high volume of air that is delivered at relatively low pressures of 2 to 10 psi to the spray gun. And, unlike the standard air compressor, HVLP turbines generate air flow from 50 to 200 scfm. Generally, turbines are available with one, two, or three stages; that is, there is a fan for each stage. The fans work in series with each other to produce higher pressures. Motor power, as listed in amperes, is critical. The greater the amperage, the greater the volume of air.

While all turbines generate air pressure and volume, the spray gun is what really defines a good HVLP system. When you are choosing an HVLP system, pay particular attention to the spray gun. Most HVLP guns are defined as "bleeder" guns; that is, air delivery is direct from the turbine via the air hose. Because there is no storage tank like a standard compressor has, air must be allowed to escape from the gun when it is not being triggered. An air valve on the gun provides an outlet so that air can constantly escape, whether or not the gun is being used. Non-bleeder guns are usually referred to as "siphon" spray guns, because the air pressure creates a partial vacuum in the cup and this draws the paint up into the gun.

For the workshop in which only a light finish or touch-up spraying is occasionally done, the single-stage turbine with approximately 7 amperes is adequate. For more viscous finishes or more continuous operation, a two- or three-stage turbine with 9 or more amperes is recommended.

A Sampling of HVLP Systems

The following are specifications for five HVLP spray systems.

depending upon the size of the air cap. (For comparison, a 3½-horsepower air compressor delivers 7 scfm at 90 psi.)

Illus. 10-2. The Accuspray model 23 HVLP spray system.

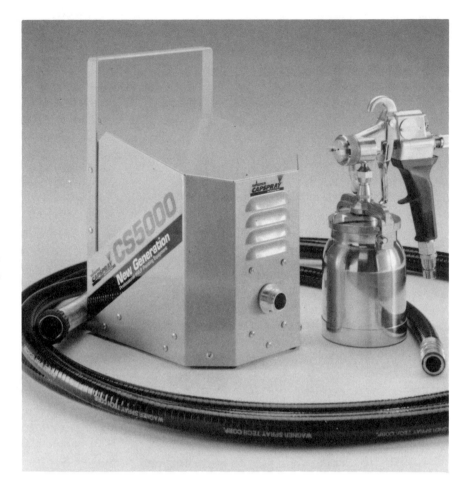

Illus. 10-3. The Wagner Spray Tech model CS5000 HVLP spray system.

Illus. 10-4. Wagner Spray Tech model Fine Coat HVLP spray system (the hose is stored inside the base compartment).

The *Accuspray model 23* spray system has a 3-stage turbine that generates an air flow of 85 cfm, and produces air that is delivered at pressures of 5 psi at the gun. The turbine has 11 amperes and runs at 110 volts. The system comes with a 25-foot-atomizing air hose and a bleeder gun. Various sizes of fluid needles, nozzles, and air caps are available.

The *Eagle Spray model ES-100* spray system has a 2-stage turbine that generates an air flow of 90 cfm, and produces air that is delivered at pressures of 5 psi at the gun. The turbine has 9.7 amperes and runs at 110 volts. The system comes with a 20-foot air hose with a 4-foot flex whip and a quick-disconnect fitting supplied with the Accuspray gun and cup. Other sizes of fluid needles, nozzles, and air caps are available.

The *Lex-Aire model LX-50A* spray system has a 2-stage turbine that generates an air flow of 60 cfm, and produces air that is delivered at pressures of 4 psi at the gun. The turbine has 8 amperes and runs at 110 volts. The system comes with a 20-foot air hose and a gun with one nozzle. Other sizes of needles and nozzles are available.

The *Wagner Capspray model CS5000* spray system has a 2-stage by-pass turbine that generates air flow of 58 cfm and produces air that is delivered at pressures of 5 psi at the gun. The turbine has 11 amperes and runs at 110 volts. It comes with a 15-foot high-flex air hose and a non-bleeder gun with one nozzle. Other sizes of fluid needles, nozzles, and air caps are available.

The *Wagner Fine Coat* spray system has a single-stage turbine that generates an air flow of 47 cfm, and produces air that is delivered at pressures of 4 psi at the gun. The turbine has 7.5 amperes and runs at 115 volts. It comes with a 15-foot flex air hose and a spray gun. It is intended for light-bodied finishes, such as stains, varnishes, lacquers, shellacs, enamels and thinned latex paint.

The *Accuspray model 23*, the *Eagle Spray model ES-1000*, the *Lex-Aire model LX-50A*, and the *Wagner Capspray model CS5000* systems are mid-sized units that are capable of spraying a variety of finishes, such as stains, lacquers and oil-based and finish-grade latex.

Whichever HVLP system is used, you must use special spray guns because the conventional compressor guns will not work on the HVLP systems. Unfortunately, there is no uniform standard which regulates the size of the openings in the air caps of the guns. Sizes vary from manufacturer to manufacturer and are identified as letters or numbers or in millimeters. The better-quality guns usually can be used with a variety of air caps for a range of purposes and finishes.

Illus. 10-5 shows a typical spray booth initially designed for a conventional spray gun, located by the large exhaust fan. The large-diameter air hose, which is routed through the wall, is the key indicator that an HVLP is now being used. The booth has an overhead florescent light and incandescent side lighting, and the walls and floor are painted white so that there is plenty of reflected light. The piece being sprayed is resting on a turntable, which makes it easy to spray all surfaces of the piece. There is also a safety waste bin for the proper disposal of solvent and paint-soaked rags.

Illus. 10-5. Spray booth with lighting, fan, and HVLP system.

An interesting accessory for the HVLP system is the turbine Aire-Booster manufactured by Lex-Aire. This unit has the operational speed of a traditional spray gun and produces the same texture-free finish as a high-pressure spray gun. The Aire-Booster increases the free-flow pressure at the spray gun two to three times, depending upon turbine size. It has a low compressed-air consumption of approximately 7 scfm and removes excess turbine heat. The Aire-Booster is available as either a wall-mounted unit or a stand-alone unit. The wall-mounted version can be installed in the spray booth which allows the turbine to be placed outside the spray area. A control feature lets you turn the turbine on and off without leaving the spray booth. And, most importantly, the Aire-Booster works with all brands of turbines and does not impair normal turbine performance.

CHAPTER ELEVEN
Hand Tools

In the past, many woodworkers earned a living by using hand tools exclusively. But today's workshop could just as easily be organized around the sole use of power tools. Power tools are easy to use, require limited training time to develop skill, and are efficient for production work. Yet hand tools still play a valuable part in the workshop. In some instances, hand tools can do a better job than the equivalent power tool. I don't know of any power tool that can even come close to producing the surface made by a well-tuned and well-sharpened hand plane.

Just about any shop, whether a general- or single-purpose shop, has an assortment of hand tools. Carvers use mallets and gouges, turners use cutting tools and calipers, model makers use fretsaws and tweezers, and the furniture maker uses planes and chisels.

Hand tools offer many advantages that are not always appreciated. As you page through today's tool catalogues that specialize in hand tools, such as the Woodcraft Supply Co. or the Garrett Wade Co. catalogues, you will find an awesome array of hand tools. And if your skill level does not include an appreciation of hand tools, you might find it difficult to know what they are used for, how to use them, how to care for them, or even how to store them.

One difference between power and hand tools is that power tools tend to be more generalized in their application. For example, table or radial arm saws can make many different types of cuts. Wood can be placed against the fence or mitre gauge and cut, regardless of grain direction or other properties. To make the same cuts with hand tools would require an array of saws and other specialized tools. It also means that the operator should have some practical training in hand tool use and sharp-ening, and some knowledge of wood properties such as grain pattern.

When purchasing a hand tool, it is sometimes difficult to judge its quality. Part of the confusion arises from the fact that tool stores and catalogues either target their merchandise at specific buyers or show every conceivable tool made. Currently, the marketing approach favored by general-purpose hardware stores is to provide tools for the "do-it-yourself" buyer. This typically means that only a limited selection of general-purpose tools such as hammers, screwdrivers, and pliers are displayed. Tool cata-logues also target specific groups of buyers: power tool users, hand tool users, lathe turners, carvers, toy makers and clock makers, to name a few. In order to have a broad perspective about the diversity of hand tools which are available, you would have to subscribe and conscien-tiously read a multitude of magazine advertisements and tool catalogues. Otherwise, there is a good chance that you will miss the tools that will best help you with your projects.

Hand-Tool Systems

In this section, hand tools are divided into groups. This is a practical method for designing storage systems and for placing tools within the shop for efficiency when working on a project. A cabinetmaker requires space for an assortment of clamps that are small and large, awk-wardly shaped and heavy. A carver needs cabinets with many drawers for storing carving tools. A turner needs a rack for storing an assortment of lathe tools conveniently near the lathe. Each of these woodworkers has unique needs and uses for hand tools. Yet the cabinetmaker also uses carving tools and the lathe turner a bench plane.

Collecting hand tools is an ongoing process. Woodworkers are always looking for a new tool either to replace a worn-out one or for a special application. The most common advice given to beginning woodworkers is to start out with a few good tools, and then add tools as interest and skills increase. But how is the beginner to know which tools to start with?

It is difficult to list the tools that are required in a shop if you consider them just general components of the shop. But if tools are organized in groups, like drill bits, measuring tools, or layout tools, then it is somewhat easier to organize a list. It also becomes easier to organize the tools for use and storage later.

The following section represents my preference in hand tools for a general-purpose workshop. Although each of these tools has a specific use and operation, its applications are commonplace and basic to most woodworking functions.

Measuring and Layout Devices

1. Awl
2. Marking knife with small blade
3. Marking gauge
4. Tape measure
5. Combination square
6. Two-, four-, and six-inch engineer squares
7. Six-, twelve-, thirty-six-, and forty-eight-inch rules
8. Circle compass or template
9. Center finder
10. Protractor
11. Level
12. T-bevel
13. Vernier caliper
14. Inside caliper
15. Outside caliper

Handsaws

1. Twenty-two–twenty-six-inch crosscut saw, 10–12 tpi (teeth per inch)
2. Twenty-two–twenty-six-inch rip saw, 5–7 tpi
3. Eight-inch dovetail saw, 20–24 tpi
4. Mitre box or tenon saw
5. Coping saw
6. Deep-throat fretsaw
7. Keyhole saw
8. Hacksaw
9. Dozuki or dovetail saw, 24–27 tpi
10. Flush-trimming saw, 22–24 tpi, no tooth set
11. Short keyhole saw

Hammers/Mallets

1. Ten- to thirty-ounce dead blow mallet
2. Ten- to thirty-ounce rip hammer
3. Ten- to thirty-ounce claw hammer
4. Tack hammer
5. Four- to thirty-two-ounce ball peen hammers
6. Twelve-ounce plastic-faced hammer
7. Three-and-a-half-pound hand-drilling hammer

Drilling Supplies for Hand and Power Tools

1. Brad-point bits in the following diameters: $\frac{1}{16}$, $\frac{1}{8}$, $\frac{3}{16}$, $\frac{1}{4}$, $\frac{5}{16}$, $\frac{3}{8}$, $\frac{7}{16}$, and $\frac{1}{2}$ inch
2. A twist bit set in sizes $\frac{1}{16}$ inch through $\frac{1}{2}$ inch
3. Countersinks in sizes $\frac{1}{2}$ and $\frac{5}{8}$ inch
4. Plug cutters in sizes $\frac{1}{4}$, $\frac{3}{8}$ and $\frac{1}{2}$ inch
5. Forstner and/or multispur bits
6. Set of stop collars

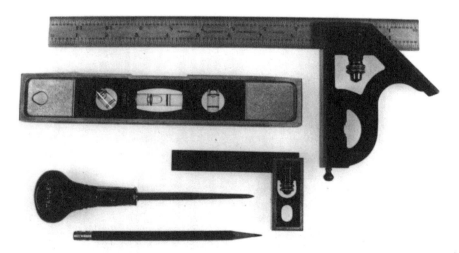

Illus. 11-1. Measuring and layout tools. From top to bottom, a combination square, level, small square, awl, and sharp pencil.

Illus. 11-2. Three types of marking gauges. At bottom is an all-metal gauge with a single point. On the left is a wood gauge with a single point on one side and two points on the other. On the right is a gauge with a longer arm and a knife blade.

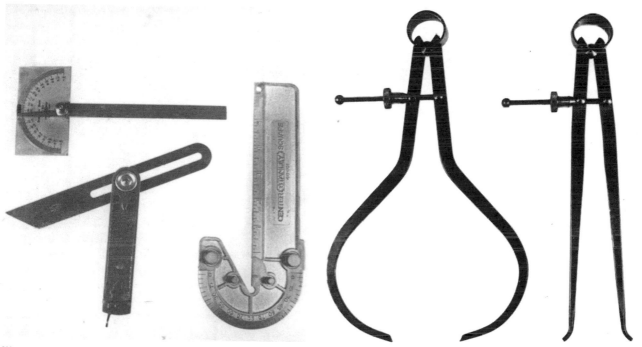

Illus. 11-3. At top is a metal protractor, on the left is a T-bevel, and on the right is a center finder.

Illus. 11-4. Inside and outside calipers.

Illus. 11-5. Rip saw (top) and crosscut saw.

Illus. 11-6. Three types of tenon saws. At the top is a Japanese saw with replaceable saw blade. In the middle is a tenon saw used in a mitre box. On the bottom is an 8-inch fine-toothed tenon saw.

Illus. 11-7. A deep-throat fretsaw (left) and a coping saw.

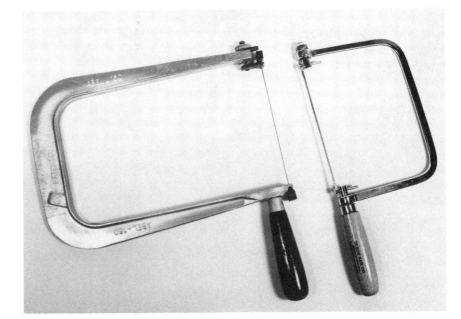

Illus. 11-8. A 3½-pound hand-drilling hammer (bottom) and a 33-ounce dead blow mallet with replaceable faces.

Illus. 11-9. A claw hammer (top), tack hammer (center), and rip hammer (bottom).

Illus. 11-10. Assorted drilling supplies. From left to right: plug cutter, multispur cutter, Forstner bit, countersink bit, brad-point bit, and twist bit. At bottom is a brad-point bit and stop collars.

Planes

The numbers listed below are for Stanley model numbers. Record Co. and other plane makers often use the same numbering system. Some planes are no longer manufactured, but can be found at auctions, flea markets and from other woodworkers.

1. No. 60½ low-angle block plane
2. No. 92 rabbet plane
3. No. 3 or 4 smooth plane
4. No. 71 router plane
5. No. 5 jack plane
6. Flat spokeshave
7. No. 6, 7, or 8 fore, trying, or jointer plane
8. No. 95 edge-trimming block plane
9. No. 78 rabbet plane
10. Japanese chamfer plane
11. No. 79 side rabbet plane
12. Round spokeshave

Chisels

Chisels are available in either inches or millimeters.
1. Bevel-edge chisels (set of eight) in sizes ⅛ to 1½ inches
2. Mortise chisels in sizes ¼, ⅜, and ½ inch
3. A ¾-inch chisel for clean-up work

Lathe Tools

1. One-quarter-inch bowl gouge
2. One-half-inch bowl gouge
3. Three-eighth-inch spindle gouge
4. Three-quarter-inch spindle gouge
5. One-eighth-inch parting tool
6. Three-eighth-inch beading tool
7. Five-eighth-inch straight scraper
8. One-inch straight scraper
9. One-inch round scraper
10. One-inch skew chisel
11. One-and-one-quarter-inch left skew chisel
12. One-and-one-quarter-inch right skew chisel

Carving Tools

1. Chip-carving knives (several styles)
2. One-quarter-inch V-tool
3. Three-eight-inch straight chisel
4. Three-quarter-inch straight chisel
5. One-quarter-inch No. 4 gouge
6. Three-eight-inch No. 4 gouge
7. One-half-inch No. 5 gouge
8. One-quarter-inch No. 7 gouge
9. One-half-inch No. 8 gouge
10. One-eighth-inch No. 9 gouge
11. Three-quarter-inch No. 9 spoon gouge
12. Carver's mallet

Illus. 11-11. Bottom left, a No. 60½ low-angle block plane. Bottom right, a No. 4 smooth plane. Top, a No. 6 fore plane.

Illus. 11-12. Wood and metal smooth planes.

Illus. 11-13. From left to right: a No. 95 trimming block plane, a No. 92 rabbet plane, a wooden chamfer plane, and a No. 79 side rabbet plane.

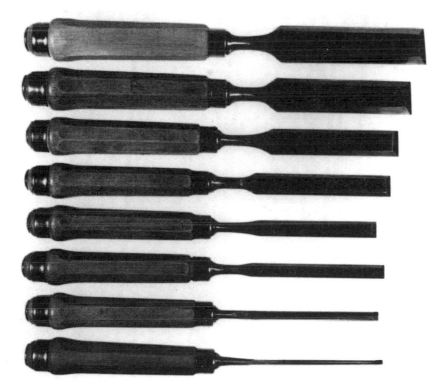

Illus. 11-14. A set of chisels. From bottom to top, the chisels are 3, 6, 10, 12, 16, 20, 26, 30 mm.

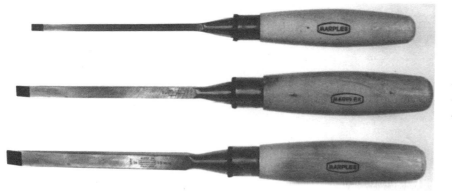

Illus. 11-15. Mortise chisels. At the bottom is a ¼-inch chisel. In the middle is a ⅜-inch chisel. At the top is a ½-inch chisel.

Illus. 11-16. Four types of chip-carving knives.

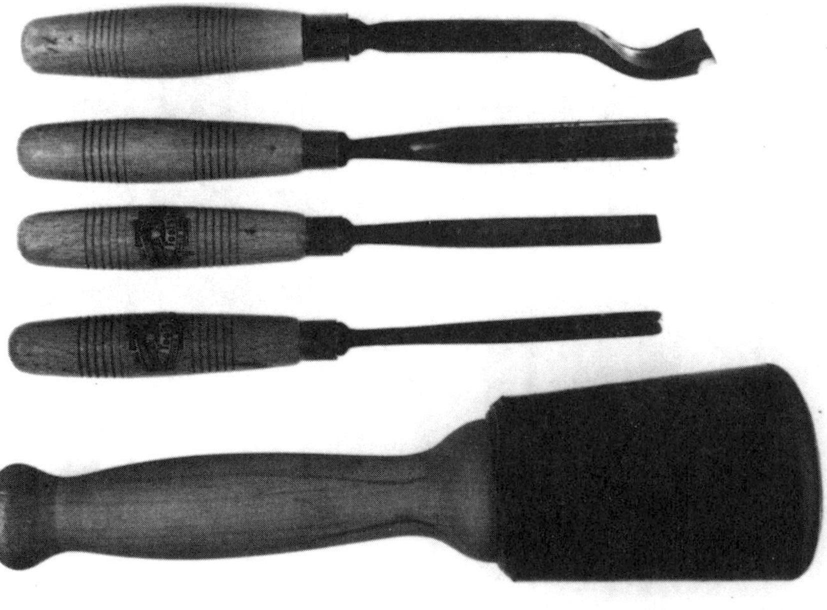

Illus. 11-17. A mallet (bottom) and assorted carving gouges.

Illus. 11-18. Bottom and center: Nicholson No. 49 and 50 rasps, which have flat and rounded sides with random tooth patterns. Top: A round rasp.

Miscellaneous Tools

1. Straight-blade screwdriver set
2. Phillips screwdriver set
3. C or G clamps
4. Band clamps
5. Bar clamps, several lengths
6. Fast or quick-action clamps, standard and deep throat
7. No. 49 and 50 Nicholson patternmaker's rasps
8. Round rasp
9. Ten-inch mill file
10. Dowelling jig
11. Bench brush

Tool Storage

This tool system was created for making average-sized furniture items. It is based upon the concept of gradation. Simply stated, it is impossible to have only one or two tools of different sizes and achieve adequate results when making a range of projects that differ in size and measurement. If you want to cut dovetails by hand, then you can either design the dovetails to match the width of a particular chisel or have a set of chisels available for use to cut a specific size and design of dovetail. Similarly, if you want to hand-plane rough lumber, then you should use a series of planes ranging from the jointer plane to the smoothing plane for best results. The concept of gradation applies equally to handsaws. A coarse-toothed ripsaw cannot be used to make picture-frame mitres or to flush-cut a dowel.

Ironically, as you do more and more of the same tasks, you will find that you gravitate to a few favorite tools. These tools are then used increasingly for an expanded number of applications. I have, for example, a full set of bench planes, but I favor a low-angle block plane and a No. 6 trying plane. In terms of workshop organization, these favorite tools tend to be the most used and are stored for quick and easy access. The least used of my planes tend to be stored farther away.

This is why there is a need for adequate tool storage which is appropriately located. Tool storage that is inadequate doesn't allow tools to be properly stored for easy access, doesn't allow space for a growing tool collection, or is a waste of precious shop space. Tool organization that is random makes it difficult to quickly find the correct tool. Tool storage that is located in either an awkward or out-of-the-way location means that time is wasted whenever you have to stop the work process to find a tool.

Design tool storage to your needs. It is a good idea to compare several different approaches to tool storage before you build. Some options are chests, cabinets, boxes and pegboards. Consider your tool selection and work habits. It is not uncommon to begin by hanging a few hand tools on a pegboard or storing them in a tool chest, and, six months later, realizing that you need a much larger or more accessible storage for a growing collection of tools.

I like to use rasps and files for many different applications, but rasps and files pose a particular problem when it comes to storage: They should never be left to rattle and bang against each other in a drawer because this damages the tool. I use many of my rasps and files without handles, so this precludes hanging them on the wall. To provide easy access for my rasps and files and still keep them separated from each other, I cut a series of ¼-inch-wide grooves in a board, place the board on a shelf near the workbench, and fit the rasps and files in the grooves.

When you are designing a tool storage system, it isn't always obvious what the work pattern or tool choice is going to be, so don't build a storage area right away. It would be better to simply place tools randomly in the shop than to build an incorrect storage system. This is a good way to determine what your specialized interests may be.

CHAPTER TWELVE

Sharpening Techniques

Sharp tools are a prerequisite for any woodworking task. Dull cutting tools, both hand and powered, are difficult and dangerous to use. Whenever I have taught classes in woodworking, whether using hand planes or table saws, I begin the class by discussing sharpening techniques.

Sharpening requires skill, good equipment, and a good work location, and is relevant to setting up the workshop. For most woodworkers, making razor-like edges is a taxing chore. Woodworkers with deficient sharpening techniques usually produce strange-looking cutting edges. Poor sharpening techniques, including not understanding what sharpness is, outdated methods, and sloppy techniques, have probably done more to ruin tools, wood, and enthusiasm than any other aspect of woodworking.

Different Perspectives

Lathe turners want cutting tools that can be power-sharpened and are resistant to heat buildup. Their key concern is how well the tool actually cuts or scrapes wood, rather than the specific cutting angle on the tool. For a turner, the ideally sharpened lathe tool removes wood efficiently and leaves a smooth surface that requires only minimal sanding.

To expedite the sharpening process, many turners are using bench grinders or powered waterwheels (Illus. 12-1 and 12-2). Illus. 12-3 and 12-4 show two simple shop-made jigs that both steady the long lathe tool and hold it at a specific angle to the grinding wheel. The handle end of the tool fits into the V-shaped stop piece which allows the tool to be smoothly rotated against the wheel. Some

Illus. 12-1. The Delta model 23-880 eight-inch bench grinder. The grinder is fastened to a board which is clamped at the end of a lathe.

Illus. 12-2. The Delta model 23-700 Universal Wet/Dry Grinder.

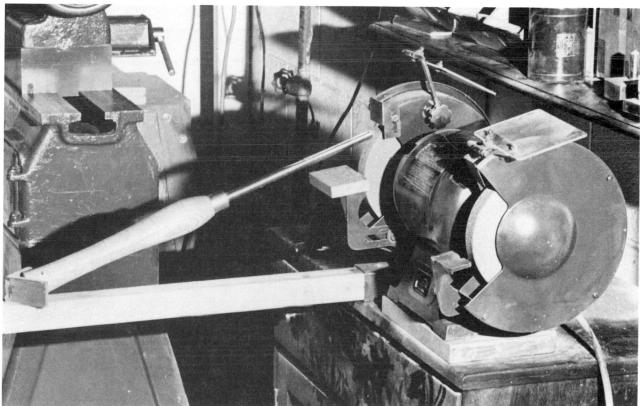

Illus. 12-0. A custom-made tool rest for sharpening lathe tools.

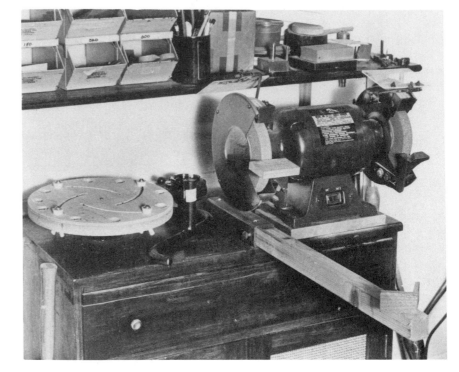

Illus. 12-4. Another custom-made tool rest. Note that a block of wood has been added to the tool rest, providing a larger work area.

turners use the sharpened tool immediately after grinding without removing the residual wire edge from the cutting edge. Others prefer to remove the wire edge by finishing the sharpening with a fine-grit stone and a strop.

Skew and scraper lathe tools are generally held by hand on the grinder tool rest against the grinding wheel. As shown in Illus. 12-4, a block of wood has been added to the tool rest to make a larger resting surface for the tools and to help keep the lathe tool well above the top half of the grinding wheel. This is important for visibility as well as for maintaining the proper edge shape of the tool. If a lathe tool is held against the grinding wheel at approximately a 10 o'clock position, the bevel that is made will angle in a traditional manner. If, however, the lathe tool is held against the wheel at or below a 9 o'clock position, the bevel will either be nonexistent or at a reverse angle. (Tools rests can be tilted to deliberately create different bevel angles.) Also note in Illus. 12-3 that the grinder is located adjacent to the lathe for easy and quick access.

Carvers use a wide assortment of knives, chisels and gouges, and it is also not uncommon for a carver to change the angle of a tool several times during a project. Carvers, much like turners, are not as concerned about specific cutting angles as they are about the ability of the tool to cut wood cleanly in all grain directions.

Carvers use so many different types of sharpening equipment that it seems difficult to list them all. Flat stones, slipstones, waterstone grinders, and narrow belt (1-inch) strip sanders are some of the systems with which I am familiar. Chip carvers often sharpen knives using a small, flat stone or with a horizontally mounted powered waterstone grinder. More important than the system used is an understanding of how to use each system as efficiently as possible. Most chisels and gouges made today have a relatively thin cross section and are composed of a carbon steel which is relatively soft. This means that if these tools are sharpened on a standard bench grinder, the steel will probably burn and detemper. But these same thin, soft-steel tools are reasonably easy to sharpen with bench stones. In fact, some tools such as the V gouge are best sharpened with bench stones.

If you do a lot of sharpening or need to adjust the edge bevel while working, using a water grinder for sharpening is probably best. The constant drip of the water on the stone helps to keep the tool from burning. However, this does not guarantee that the tool won't burn. When using power grinders, develop the technique of moving the cutting edge of the tool lightly over the grinder.

One simple test for determining if a tool is sharp is to use a block of wood that is the same as the project wood to test the cutting tool. Use the sharpened tool to make cuts across the grain, with the grain, and on the end grain. If the tool is properly sharpened, it shouldn't tear the grain. Rather, there should be a shearing sound and the waste pieces should be cleanly formed. If not, either change the bevel angle of the tool or touch up the edges with a fine-grit stone until the tool cuts correctly.

Cabinetmakers and furniture makers have a different perspective about sharpening than turners and carvers. It's generally agreed that a narrow range of specific cutting angles is required. Despite the variety of planes and chisels, the shapes and angles of a cabinetmaker's cutting blades are more standardized than those of a turner or carver.

Perhaps it's because of chisel and plane blade similarities that cabinetmakers usually don't modify the cutting angles of their tools as much as turners and carvers. Some, however, are greatly concerned with finding the correct cutting angle. But this is often difficult. Consider, for example, trying to hold a cutting tool on a flat stone, at a specific angle, while moving it back and forth at a specific angle. Maybe these cabinetmakers should take the same approach to sharpening as carvers and turners.

One of the advantages of modern technology is that we can approach our sharpening work with greater precision. Knowing the grit size of a stone should allow us to use stones in systematic ways. With the use of sharpening and honing guides, there is a more reliable method to guarantee a repeatable angle on a cutting tool. All this should enhance our ability to repeatedly sharpen a tool to the same sharpness it was before it became dull, or modify the cutting edge of a tool to a specific angle for use with different types of wood.

My Sharpening System

In the ideal workshop, a specific location would be set up for sharpening. The sharpening work station would include a 3 × 6-foot water- and oil-proof work surface, complete with a metal vise and plenty of cabinet and drawer space. This work station, of course, would be adjacent to a sink and running water.

In lieu of having the perfect work station, I use a more portable arrangement. The grinder I use for sharpening lathe tools is located next to the lathe, and the rest of my sharpening equipment is stored in a small cabinet and a single drawer. When it's time to sharpen my tools, I use a corner of my bench to set up my equipment (Illus. 12-5).

I have experimented with just about every available sharpening device and system. I've used oil and waterstones, diamond stones, steel plates and grit powders, felt and lather strops, hand- and foot-powered wheel grinders, bench grinders, waterstone grinders, belt sanders, a variety of guides, and even sandpapers. The fundamental lesson I've learned is that it's best to establish a system that is easy, quick, and efficient. Another lesson learned is that there isn't one single combination stone that can produce a sharp edge. To achieve the ultimate edge requires a stepping-stone approach to sharpening. My method, which employs an electric waterstone grinder, a honing guide, a series of waterstones, and a strop, allows me to sharpen and hone a dull edge to unbelievable sharpness in minutes.

Illus. 12-5. A sharpening work station for chisels and planes. The work surface is secured in a vise and the waterstones are stored in a bucket of water. Note the honing guides, a protractor, a 6-inch rule, rags, and a spray can of oil for rust prevention.

To sharpen my 10-inch planer blades, I set a Makita waterstone grinder at the corner of the bench, extend a plastic hose from it to a bucket on the floor, and pour water from a plastic jug into the water reservoir. In less than five minutes, a dull planer knife can be sharpened. If the knife has a nick or is extremely dull, I start with a 120-grit silicon-carbide wheel and then complete the process with the standard 1,000-grit wheel.

I use flat bench stones to sharpen and hone all my plane and chisel blades. I never use a bench power grinder on any chisel or plane blade. A power grinder may be quick and fast, but can retemper (color it blue), remove too much steel, or leave coarse grinder scratches. If a cutting tool is exceptionally dull or damaged, I sometimes use a power waterstone grinder for the preliminary shaping. In fact, I made an auxiliary work surface so that the honing guide can be used with the water grinder. This method allows the blade edge to move straight towards the center of the waterstone (Illus. 12-6 and 12-7).

As a waterstone revolves, it varies slightly in rpm from

Illus. 12-6. The Makita waterstone grinder with a custom-made platform for the honing guide.

Illus. 12-7. The platform in use. The cutting edge is kept parallel to the waterstone rotation.

its center to the outer edge. If a cutting edge is placed so that its corner edges are pointing towards the center and the outer edge of the wheel, the difference in rpm will cause the cutting edge to be sharpened with a skewed angle. The auxiliary work surface enables the honing guide to cross over the rotating stone, which minimizes the distortion caused by variations in rpm. Remember, this system is used only for preliminary work.

When choosing natural or man-made stones, there are several factors to consider other than particle size. These include stone hardness, ease in reflattening the stone, the tendency of the stone to clog up with solvent and cutting debris, availability of different grit sizes, and cost.

After critically comparing the performance of oilstones and waterstones, I decided to use waterstones. Waterstones are man-made stones which are composed of compressed rare earths, ceramics, or finely ground natural rock. They have many advantages over natural oilstones. Their grit size is measurable and consistent throughout the stone, and stones are available in a wide variety of grit sizes, ranging from 80 to 8000 grit. By comparison, the grit of the black, hard Arkansas stone is twice as large as the grit of the 4000-grit waterstone. Waterstones are relatively "soft" so they wear down quickly, which exposes fresh grit particles, and are easily reflattened. Water is safer and healthier to use as a stone lubricant than either oils or solvents. Waterstones can be cut and reshaped so that unusually shaped tools can be sharpened, and are wide enough to sharpen plane blades. And lastly, waterstones are reasonably priced; basic waterstones are approximately one-third the cost of 8000-grit polishing stones.

When using my sharpening stones, I place a 2 × 2-foot piece of wood on the bench. This wood piece has a cleat for securing it in the front vise, and low strips of wood around its perimeter to keep water off the bench. The wood strips function as a splash guard, but they are by no means watertight. Remember, however, that it isn't necessary to keep waterstones sopping wet during use.

At one time, I kept the man-made waterstones in a bucket in a laundry sink that the water softener system purged itself into every other day. This ensured that there was a constant cleaning and freshening of the water. In over five years, the stones never dissolved or accumulated mineral deposits. However, never leave natural rock nagura stones and natural finish stones in water because they will decompose. I no longer have running water or a sink in the shop, so I let the stones dry between use and only soak them for about 10 minutes before using them. I keep the polishing stones separate from the coarser stones, so no stray grit particles can contaminate the polishing stones.

Early on in my quest for a sharpening system, I flattened the coarser stones on my concrete shop floor. Now, whenever a hollow develops in the stones, I use 3M sandpaper to flatten them. It is much easier, neater, and controllable.

Honing Guides

There are many types of honing guides. The Eclipse and Veritas guides are very good because they can be easily adjusted to a specific angle and they roll on the stone. This makes it easy to go from stone to stone and guarantee the same angle. Guides which have rollers that roll on the workbench have to be readjusted for each stone. The Eclipse honing guide grips the tool's edges. This is fine for bevel-edged chisels and plane blades, but not for large mortise chisels or ⅛-inch-wide chisels. The Veritas honing guide is good for most tools, skewed blades, or thick chisels like mortise chisels. It also has a cam-type roller for setting a range of secondary angles.

Grooving the stones with the roller need not be a problem, if proper technique is used. For the forward stroke, simply place both thumbs under the blade, behind the guide, and near the roller. Both index fingers should be on the tool surface near the cutting edge. Apply even pressure downward with your fingers and let your thumbs push the guide forward. (Don't apply any downward pressure with your thumbs.) For the return stroke, lessen the downward pressure, bring the guide back, and repeat the forward pressure stroke. After use, the honing guides can be cleaned with a light oil like WD-40.

Honing guides are principally designed for bevel-edged chisels and plane blades. These tools are generally difficult to hold the sharpening area flush against a stone by hand because of their relative thinness (³⁄₁₆ inch or less) and the small surface area of the blade.

Thicker (¼- to ½-inch) chisel and plane blades, such as mortise chisels and most Japanese chisels and plane blades, may not fit in some honing guides. Instead, a different type of honing guide must be used, although the style that is designed with opposing handles and a single tightening screw for securing the chisel sometimes allows the blade to pivot at the screws, which results in a skewed shape. Because of their thickness, the bevel on these chisels and blades has sufficient surface area so that the tools can be held flat upon a stone by hand.

I use a small 4-inch square to check that the cutting edge is straight and square with the side of the blade.

With either the Eclipse or Veritas honing guides, an engineer's protractor (made of metal) can be used for setting the bevel angle relative to the honing guide roller. An alternative method is to use a 6-inch rule (Eclipse guide only) to set the projection of the cutting edge as indicated by the legend marked on the side of the guide. For the Veritas guide, use the company's angle jig which was especially designed for this purpose.

Many times, woodworkers do not take the sharpening process far enough. If the grit scratches or the wire edge which is left over from sharpening are not removed, a chisel or plane blade can't hold an edge (assuming proper bevel angles, etc.).

The wire edge, which isn't visible with the naked eye, will still be present even after an 8000-grit stone has been used. If the wire edge is not removed, it can microscopically tear back bevel steel and accelerate dullness. If two identical chisels are sharpened and honed with 8000-grit stones, the one which is further honed with the buffing rouge will hold an edge considerably longer than the one which is not.

Backs and Bevels

Both the bevel and back of chisel and plane blades must be properly prepared. Too often, the bevel is impeccably honed and the back is ignored. This causes the tool to dull quickly as it is used, and before long the woodworker is once again looking for a better brand of cutting tool.

Unless the back is flattened and polished, the irregularities caused by factory grinding will show up at the cutting edge. New chisels and plane blades usually have a variety of wavy-shaped backs. At the factory, the steel may have been buffed so that the edge is rounded towards the bevel face, or grinding scratches may come through to the cutting bevel and cause the edge to look like a serrated knife. Before using a new chisel, attempt to flatten the back on an 800-grit stone. If it looks like a lot of steel needs to be removed (from the cutting edge back about 2 inches), begin flattening with a 120-grit stone. If not, continue with the 800-grit stone through the various grit sizes to the polish stones.

Many different techniques are advocated for sharpening the bevel side of the cutting blade. The fact is that different woods and cutting techniques are going to influence how a tool will cut and for how long it will stay sharp. The wood, bevel angle, steel quality, whether the tool is used with the hand or a mallet, and the types of cuts made will affect the cutting edge. Teak wears a cutting edge differently than pine, and light paring cuts aren't as forceful as a mallet-driven mortise cut.

It would be nice to have a chart which is applicable to all blades and woods, but one doesn't exist. However, several general guidelines can be given. For light paring chisels that are used only by hand (no mallet), use a 15- to 25-degree angle. For standard bench chisels and plane blades, use bevels from 20 to 30 degrees. Mortise chisels may require bevel angles from 25 to 40 degrees.

Here's a simple test that will aid you in determining bevel angles. Mark out a ⅜-inch-wide mortise approximately 1 inch deep in maple, fir, and pine. Using a mortise chisel with a 25-degree bevel, begin to cut the mortises. As you hold the chisel perpendicular to the work surface and hit it with a mallet, note if the chisel leans over as you drive it into the wood despite your efforts to maintain it at 90 degrees. If the chisel leans, resharpen it to a different angle and try the mortise cut again. Repeat the sharpening process, until the chisel no longer leans when it is hit. You may find that there is a different ideal bevel angle for every wood.

After preparing the bevel, many woodworkers stop the sharpening process. The main drawback to stopping at this point is that the entire bevel will have to be resharpened or rehoned when the blade dulls. For this reason, it is advisable to make a secondary angle upon the main bevel edge. This makes the edge slightly thicker and stronger and more resistant to breakage. Also, honing a dulled edge with a secondary bevel is faster because a smaller amount of steel has to be removed. The angle of the secondary bevel can be determined by trial and error and may vary from 2 to 10 degrees. For example, hone a 5-degree secondary bevel and then use the tool. If it works properly, fine. If not, hone it again at either 3 or 7 degrees. Use the mortise test described above and change the secondary angle until the chisel cuts without leaning, or has the least cutting resistance. Keep records of the various secondary angles for different woods.

Secondary angles are another reason to use honing guides. It is simple to set a secondary angle using a honing guide, and a honing guide also makes it easier to return to a specific angle or change to a different angle. My rule of thumb is that when the secondary bevel is about ⅛ inch wide, I reshape the main bevel and put on a new secondary bevel.

The final step in honing plane blades is to nick off the blade corners by rubbing them at an angle to the side of the stone. This will prevent a misaligned plane blade from digging into the workpiece.

Equipment for Sharpening

My choices for sharpening equipment are as follow:

1. Eclipse and/or Veritas honing guides
2. Waterstones in the following grits: 120 (Naniwa brand), 800, 1200, 4000, 8000 (King brand)
3. Scrubbing (nagura) stones for the 4000 and 8000 stones
4. Sanding screen (medium-grit, silicon-carbide 3M)
5. Green or buffing honing rouge
6. Leather strop and/or 6-inch hard-felt buffing wheel
7. 4-inch square
8. 6-inch steel rule
9. Protractor or other device for setting angles

For the woodworker who sharpens tools infrequently and wants an inexpensive system, the initial set should consist of 120-, 800-, and 1200-grit stones and the Eclipse honing guide. Otherwise, I use the 120-, 800-, 1200-, 4000- and 8000-grit stones and buffing rouge because it's really more efficient to use the various stones than to attempt the entire sharpening process on one or two stones.

Sharpening Stones

The various grit stones are going to stay wet differently. The 120-grit stone will seem to continuously drain water away, whereas the 8000-grit stone will seem to resist getting wet. The best method is to keep the surfaces wet, but not flooded. Also, don't wipe off the water and slurry while working, because the slurry is actually part of the sharpening process. Slurry is composed of worn grit and steel particles, so it acts as a lubricant and polish. In fact, when you are almost finished with a particular stone, add no more water and continue using it until the slurry is dry (ease up on the downward pressure at the same time). This will act as a transition step to the next stone.

The 120-grit stone is used primarily for the quick removal of steel. Use it, for example, when first shaping a bevel angle or removing a break or large nick. The 120-grit stone can also be used for initially resurfacing chisel and plane backs which are very uneven.

The 800-grit stone is used to remove the scratches left by the 120-grit stone. Not only is the 800-grit stone a good stone to use when a tool is very dull, but it is also useful for removing minor nicks. And the 800-grit stone can also be used to flatten the backs of chisels and plane blades if they are not too uneven.

The 1200-grit stone is used after the 800-grit stone, after the tool back is flattened and the main bevel is made.

Many times, I have made five to ten passes on this stone with a dull blade and gone on to the polish stones.

At this stage, one could end the sharpening and honing process because the surface finish is adequate for general-purpose tool use. However, once you have used polishing stones, you will be so delighted with the polished, chrome-like surfaces that it will be impossible to ever be happy with partly finished tools again.

By the time the blade has been refined with the 1,200-grit stone, it only takes a few strokes on each stone to finish the secondary bevel. Once the secondary bevel is finished, turn the blade over and make several passes across the back with the two polishing stones to remove most of the residue wire edge.

The 4000- and 8000-grit stones and green rouge are used to refine the cutting edge. The back of the blade should be finished through to the 8000-grit stone. Only the secondary bevel should be honed further with the green rouge.

The 4000- and 8000-grit stones have similar characteristics; it's a matter of degree how they refine the edge. Both will require the use of a small, hand-sized scrubbing stone called a nagura stone. Rubbing this on the polishing stone will create a muddy-looking slurry and clean away the stone's bonding agent and metal residue. The slurry will also aid in the polishing of the blade. Polishing stones are relatively soft, so it is easy to gouge them. Be careful with the forward and rearward stroking.

The Ultimate Edge

Removing the wire edge is the final process in achieving a sharp tool. This can be done in several ways. If the tool has an odd-shaped edge, such as a V-carving chisel, a corner chisel or an in-cannel gouge, use a piece of flexible leather with either the rouge or a fine aluminum oxide powder. The second method requires using a buffing wheel on a slow-speed motor. To remove the micro-wire edge, lightly touch the secondary bevel to a hard-felt wheel and green gouge. One or two light passes on the wheel are enough; be sure to keep the bevel parallel to the wheel. For powered buffing wheels, use grinders with motor speeds less than 1800 rpm (Illus. 12-8). The wheel on the left side of the buffer in Illus. 12-8 is a rubber wheel with a 3-inch-wide aluminum oxide sanding belt. The wheel has diagonally cut slots through the rubber part just under the sanding belt. When the motor is turned on, the wheel enlarges due to centrifugal force and holds the belt in place. The sanding belt fits loosely on the wheel when it isn't turning. This makes it easy to

Illus. 12-8. A Baldor ¼-horsepower buffer with an expandable wheel with an abrasive belt (left side) and hard felt wheel (right side). Also shown are a sewn muslin wheel, a rake to remove wax glaze on the muslin wheel, and a block of rouge.

change to different grit belts. Use the wheel to sharpen carving tools, drawknives, and other tools that are difficult to sharpen on flat stones.

One shop accessory that has always been difficult to sharpen is drill bits. I'm sure that many shop workers have overused bits until the bits turned black from too much use and too little (if any) sharpening, and then purchased new drill bits instead of sharpening the old ones. This can become expensive and is not really necessary because drill bits can be easily resharpened using a jig. The Dremel Co. has an accessory which fits onto its model 1731 disc belt sander which makes sharpening drill bits easy (Illus. 12-9 and 12-10).

Chart 12-1 shows relative particle (grit) sizes of different sharpening products.

Stone (grit or Name)	Particle Size (Microns)
60X	270
Coarse India	173
100 X	150
280 X	150
600 X	29
Fine India	23
800 X (King)	20
1000 X (King)	16
1200 X (King)	13
Soft Arkansas	13
Hard Arkansas	10
Washita	8
Black Hard Arkansas	5
4000 X (King models S-1 and S-2)	2
8000 X (King models G-1 and G-2)	1
Buffing compound (green)	0.5

Chart 12-1.

Illus. 12-9. The Dremel model 1731 disc/belt sander.

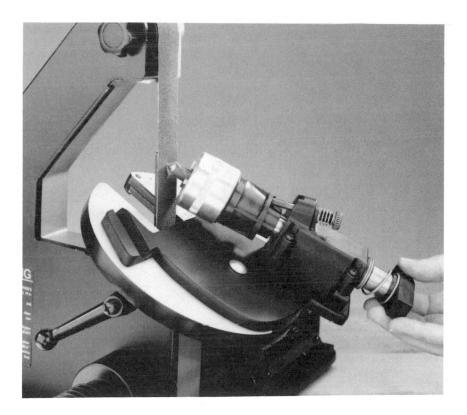

Illus. 12-10. The drill bit sharpening attachment for the Dremel sander.

CHAPTER THIRTEEN
Jigs and Fixtures

I once attended an auction of a workshop that had been owned by a fellow who had been doing woodworking for 40 or 50 years. There were many fine old tools and racks of beautiful lumber. The auction was quite crowded and everyone was enthusiastically bidding and buying. After it was over, the only things left were a pile of seemingly unrecognizable odds and ends. Upon closer examination, these objects turned out to be jigs and fixtures. No one had wanted them probably because it was not readily apparent what the jigs at the auction were made to do. A jig or fixture is a device made to assist in a particular woodworking procedure. Jigs are made of practically any material and either can be "cobbled" together or made with furniture-like precision. In this chapter, I describe jigs and fixtures that can be of great help in the workshop.

Bench Hooks

The bench hook is one of two bench accessories that I have found to be extremely useful. Not only is it simple to make, but it helps you perform precise work.

The bench hook can be used with either a block plane or a fine-tooth saw. The bench hook is "hooked" on the edge of the bench, as shown in Illus. 13-1 and 13-2, and

Illus. 13-1. A bench hook used for accurate sawing.

Illus. 13-2. This bench hook is used with a block plane to square the board edge.

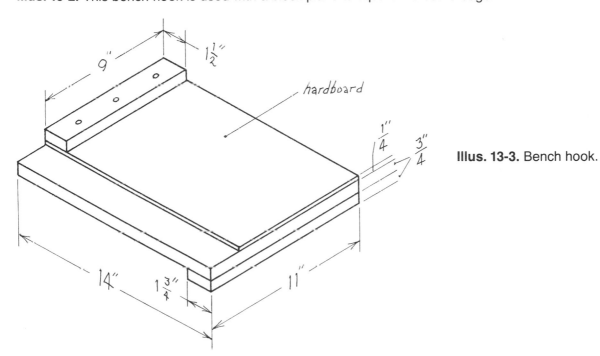

Illus. 13-3. Bench hook.

the workpiece is hand-held or toggle-clamped against the wooden stop block. The layer of hardboard creates a gap between the workpiece and the lower piece of plywood. This gap allows the plane to slide against the lower piece of plywood for planing work, and also provides a gap so that when it's used as a sawing platform, the bench hook is not scarred badly. The most critical element in constructing a bench hook is the angle at which the wooden stop block is attached; it must be precisely 90 degrees. (But you can also make bench hooks with stop blocks at other angles for mitre work.)

Shooting Boards

My other favorite bench accessory is the shooting board. It is made of two long pieces of wood, a block of wood and a drywall screw, and can actually be used instead of the jointer. You can make the shooting board any length (Illus. 13-4), but it's reasonable to make it as long as your bench. To use the shooting board, place your workpiece so that it overhangs the top and lies against the stop block and catches on the point of the screw. Lay a fore, jack or smooth plane on its side and move it along the edge of the workpiece to plane (Illus. 13-5).

The shooting board can be further varied by adding a "ramp" to the surface on which the plane slides. As the plane is slid uphill upon the angled surface, the entire width of the plane blade is used. This ensures that the edge of the plane blade is worn evenly.

Using a plane with a shooting board can be uncomfortable if you are doing a considerable amount of work. At one time, special planes were made specifically for use with shooting boards. Record Company's T-5 technical jack plane, although no longer manufactured, was one. It was similar to a standard jack plane except a wooden handle could be threaded on to either of it's sides. This made the plane very comfortable to use with a shooting board. You can make your own shooting board by modifying a standard jack plane. Simply tap screw holes into the sides and attach a shop-made handle. (Do not do this with antique planes because of their intrinsic and historic value.)

Illus. 13-4 (right). Three sizes of shooting boards.

Illus. 13-5. Using a Record T-5 plane to square a board edge on the shooting board.

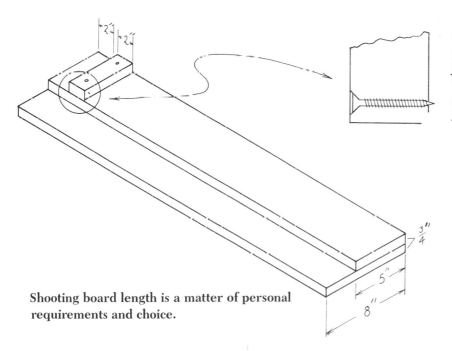

Cross Section of Stop Block

Note that drywall screw projects slightly from block.

The screw head is deeply countersunk so that the projecting point is adjustable.

Illus. 13-6.

Shooting board length is a matter of personal requirements and choice.

Other Jigs and Accessories

Another useful bench tool, especially if you enjoy using a hand plane, is the bevel-planing jig shown in Illus. 13-7. The workpiece is placed in the jig against an adjustable backstop, and the backstop is secured by a single wedge.

The workpiece is held against one side of the jig by hand (Illus. 13-9), and, as the plane rides on the upper brace and the lower edge of the jig, the workpiece is planed to the desired bevel.

A simple mitre box, with one side extended so that it can be held in the front vise, is another practical bench

Illus. 13-7. A custom-made bevel planing jig being used with a No. 5 jack plane.

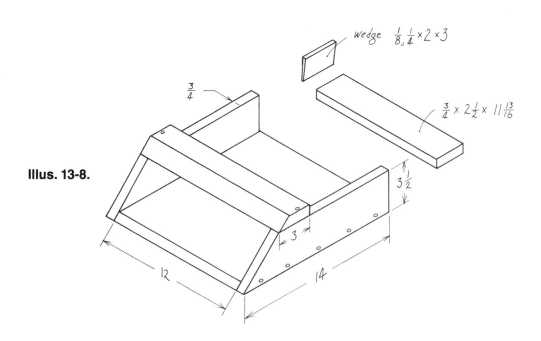

Illus. 13-8.

Illus. 13-9. Using the bevel-planing jig.

Illus. 13-10. A mitre box secured in a vise. Note that wedges secure the workpiece in the mitre box.

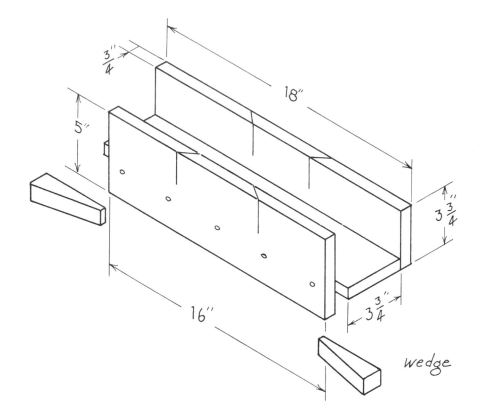

Illus. 13-11. Mitre box.

Illus. 13-12. A tray for sorting and pouring small parts, screws, nuts, washers, etc.

accessory that is very easy to make (Illus. 13-10). The workpiece rests within the box and is secured at either end with wedges. This is a very handy jig, and since it is so simple to make, it is easy to make different jigs for 45, 90, and 22½ degrees, or any other angle.

Illus. 13-12 shows a small tray used in the workshop to sort small parts and "pour" them back into their containers. The hole is for hanging the tray next to the hardware shelves.

Dean Slindee keeps a couple of pails of incremental sticks handy in his shop (Illus. 13-13). The maple sticks are 10 inches long, and range in width from .04 inch to 1¼ inches in increments of .01 inch. They are used as spacers and for measuring and calibrating various setup procedures. For example, if a dado has to be cut exactly 1 inch from a previous cut, the 1-inch stick is used to offset the workpiece from the fence by 1 inch. Or, if a ¹⁄₁₆-inch rabbet has to be cut, the ¹⁄₁₆-inch spacer can be temporarily glued onto the out-feed side of the router table. When the workpiece is cut, it will be supported by the spacer as it exits the router cutter. Dean also made a jig to hold the sticks while he stamped the sizes on each (Illus. 13-14). The stick is placed in a trough and into a block with a square hole. The stick is positioned by a stop which is adjustable for single- or double-digit numbers. Steel number punches are then used to mark the stick size.

Dean also made an adjustable jig that he uses to make accurate mitre cuts on the table saw (Illus. 13-15). A plywood table was fitted with two runners which fit into the mitre grooves of the table saw. (If you do not want to use wood for runners because it swells and contracts during the different seasons, you can use metal Incra Miter Sliders.) The mitre tabletop can be any size; just be certain there is sufficient support area for stability and working. The two mitre fences are adjustable by T-slot fittings. This provides ample workpiece support both close and far from the saw blade. Note the left-side mitre fence in Illus. 13-15. The workpiece is clamped to the fence, and a piece of paper is placed between the fixed and adjustable parts of the fence. The paper shim is the final calibrating element and guarantees a perfect 45-degree cut.

Dean also uses two sets of different-width, height-adjustable sawhorses (Illus. 13-16 and 13-17). The sawhorses are made of hard maple and consist of two main parts. The lower legs have four wing bolts through the stretchers. The upper support has T slots cut into the vertical pieces. By loosening the wing nuts, you can raise or lower the upper part.

Norm Peterson uses a different type of supporting structure in his shop. He processes quite a lot of wood through the stationary belt sander, so he has made an adjustable table that can be raised or lowered to accept

Illus. 13-13. Incremental layout and positioning sticks. They range in size from .04 to 1¼ inches in increments of .01 inch.

Illus. 13-14. A custom-made jig for stamping sizes onto incremental sticks.

Illus. 13-15. A custom-made mitre jig for a table saw.

Illus. 13-16. A set of adjustable sawhorses.

Illus. 13-17. Adjustable-height sawhorses.

wood coming from the sander by turning a hand crank (Illus. 13-18). The table is similar to the "scissor" jack used for raising automobiles.

To make round tenons on chair and stool rungs, Norm made a tenoning jig for use with a router (Illus. 13-19). The jig is clamped to the edge of a bench, and the

Illus. 13-18. An adjustable-height table. The crank raises or lowers the table.

Illus. 13-19. A round-tenon cutting jig.

Illus. 13-20. A close-up of the round-tenon jig, workpiece, plastic guide, and router with guide bushing.

workpiece is clamped within the jig. The router guide bushing is placed in the hole in the round plastic disc (Illus. 13-20). The router cutter is lowered the correct distance, and the router and disc are turned around the workpiece.

Because Norm does production work, he often finds it necessary to modify machines for quicker setups. His favorite device is an air cylinder. The bench drill press shown in Illus. 13-21 has a pneumatic cylinder fitted to the quill. After the operator places the workpiece against the table guides, he uses a foot switch to activate the cylinder for lowering and raising the drill bit.

Another example of a pneumatic cylinder is the horizontal boring machine (shown in Illus. 13-22). A special carriage was made to hold the workpiece. When a switch is activated, the drill motor turns on, and the air cylinder advances the drill a specified distance and then retracts the bit.

Tom Zumbach specializes in lathe turning and his jigs reflect that interest. He made a metal frame to glue up laminations for bowl blanks (Illus. 13-23). The wood pieces are stacked on the bottom surface of the frame, and a hydraulic jack is used to press the pieces together.

Tom's drum sander, while not a classic jig, is a shop-made tool (Illus. 13-24 and 13-25). Workpieces are manually pushed under the drum, and the wooden hand wheel is used to raise or lower the sanding table.

The Hitachi compound mitre saw in Jim Kirchner's shop is fitted with a shop-made fence (Illus. 13-26). The fence has stick-on measuring tape and drop stops for

Illus. 13-21. This drill press has a pneumatic cylinder and a foot control petal for raising and lowering the drill press quill.

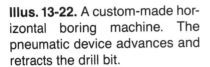 **Illus. 13-22.** A custom-made horizontal boring machine. The pneumatic device advances and retracts the drill bit.

Illus. 13-23. A custom-made frame and hydraulic jack used to clamp lathe-work laminations.

Illus. 13-24. A custom-made drum sander. The dust hood with plastic front is removed to reveal the drum.

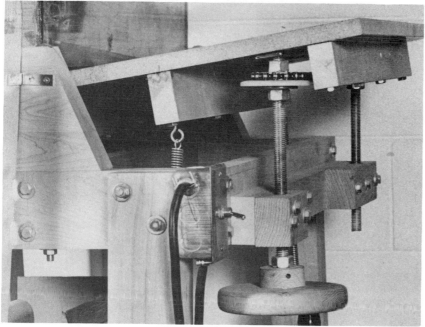

Illus. 13-25. A close-up of the table-adjustment mechanism on the drum sander.

Illus. 13-26. This Hitachi compound mitre saw has a custom-made fence, drop stops, and a roller stand.

accurate cutting. The fence also rests upon a roller stand, so that longer workpieces are easy to move.

Illus. 13-27 shows an oversized table that is bolted to the scroll saw to make it easier to support larger workpieces over the table area and to support smaller pieces close to the blade. The top is made of cabinet-grade birch plywood that was sanded smooth and finished with Danish oil and several coats of wax. Often the slot in the scroll saw table is too large for small workpieces, which makes it dangerous or impossible to hold these pieces unsupported at the blade. The table insert (Illus. 13-28) allows easy blade changes while providing table support at the blade.

Anvils are not that common anymore. But if you are fortunate to find or have one, the traditional method of supporting the anvil is with a section of a log (Illus.

Illus. 13-27 (above left). An oversized table bolted to the scroll saw. **Illus. 13-28 (above right).** A close-up of the table insert in the scroll-saw table. The fibreboard piece has a small hole so that smaller workpieces can be placed and held near the blade.

Illus. 13-29 (above). A heavy anvil on a traditional section of log. **Illus. 13-30 (right).** This anvil placed on a "log" is made of nailed and glued-up pieces of framing studs.

13-29). I was fortunate to obtain an anvil, but I do not have access to logs and stumps. So I made a "log" out of thirty-two 2-foot lengths of 2 × 4 studs that I glued and nailed together for rigidity (Illus. 13-30).

The Leigh dovetail jig is normally fastened to a board that is then clamped to the workbench. This is satisfactory as long as the workpiece will fit between the jig and the floor. Illus. 13-31 shows a box (36 × 12 × 7½ inches) that is used to "extend" the distance between floor and jig. The box can be easily clamped to the workbench for use, and then hung on a wall peg when not in use. The only limitation on box height is your ability to safely reach the jig.

The Blade Runner II, a commercial device, is a saw and router guide that works best if it is used on a bench, cabinet top, or table. Using the Blade Runner, it's possible to cut or rout material up to 27 inches wide, which means that a 24 × 96-inch sheet of plywood can be positioned for crosscutting or cutting dadoes. (Material of this size and weight should be supported if the cuts are to be accurate.) The Blade Runner II is useful enough to warrant it's own bench, so that any number of cutting appli-

cations can be performed. Illus. 13-32 and 13-33 show a plain box with a plastic-laminated top. An extension wing—perhaps a dropleaf or roller stand—as well as lockable wheels and a storage compartment could be added for more versatility. The side benefit of adding storage is that it would make the cabinet heavier and more stable.

Another type of jig is used with the table saw. The two simple jigs shown in Illus. 13-34 are specialized wooden devices which attach to the mitre gauge. One is used to cut finger joints, and the other to cut slots in small box corners. Both devices have an indexing pin for referencing the workpiece for repetitive cuts, and both devices are attached with screws to the metal strip sitting to the left side of the mitre gauge. The metal strip is then attached to the mitre gauge.

The more elaborate box is sitting in a jig with a 45-degree V-channel. Note the location of a small pin in the channel. The box is first placed against the pin and a shallow cut is made with the table saw. The kerf cut in the box is then placed over the pin and a second cut is made. This step is repeated until all cuts are made. The spacing

Illus. 13-31. The Leigh Dovetail Jig is secured to a spacer box. This gives more distance between the jig and floor so that longer workpieces can be dovetailed.

Illus. 13-32. A Blade Runner cutting guide with a circular saw mounted to the cabinet.

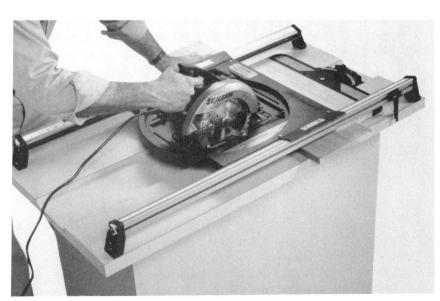

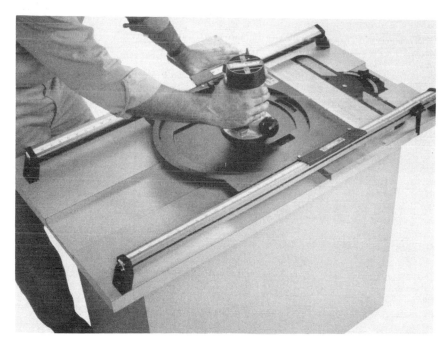

Illus. 13-33. A Blade Runner cutting guide with a router mounted to the cabinet.

Illus. 13-34 (below). At left are two different wooden faces that attach to the mitre gauge. The V block is used to cut incremental shallow cuts for splines, and the other jig is used to cut finger joints.

between cuts is a matter of choice. Whatever the spacing is between the pin and the first cut will dictate the spacing of all further cuts.

The wooden device for making finger joints is shown with a workpiece already cut. To use the device, you have to attach it to the mitre gauge and precisely calibrate it. To do this, adjust the device so that the space between the finger and the cutting blade is exactly the width of the cutter. Once the calibration is set, place the workpiece against the pin and make the first cut. Then pin the notch in the workpiece over the pin and repeat this procedure until all cuts are made. (Normally, a ¼-, ⅜-, or ½-inch slot or dado cutter is used. The jig will also work on router tables that have mitre gauge slots.)

CHAPTER FOURTEEN
Safety Procedures

Safety should always be the first consideration when working in the workshop. Woodworking involves techniques and equipment that, if improperly used, can lead to accidents. Fortunately, you can create a safe workshop environment and a method of working that permits both creative and safe work.

Before using tools and equipment, read the owner's manuals provided by the manufacturer and familiarize yourself with all safety features, procedures and warnings. Also, recognize and understand all parts and components of each tool in the workshop.

The size of a workshop and the type of woodworking performed directly affect workshop safety. Obviously, using a fretsaw to make marquetry is safer than using a table saw and shaper in a cabinet shop. However, there still are fundamental safety rules that should be followed. The following is a list of *some* general precautions and safety considerations for working in the workshop.

1. Don't work when you are tired.
2. Never work under the influence of alcohol, drugs, or medications.
3. Wear proper work clothing. Do not wear loose clothing.
4. Remove all jewelry, ties, and scarfs, and tie up long hair.
5. If possible, do not work if no one else is nearby.
6. Unplug electrical tools and machines when making adjustments and attaching accessories.
7. Do not work with a cluttered floor.
8. Have proper lighting and ventilation.
9. Use all machine safety guards.
10. When using solvents, finishing products or other chemicals, read the labels for all warnings.
11. The electrical power and wiring in the workshop should be sufficient to operate all machines safely.
12. Use tools and machines only for their intended purposes.
13. Be certain that any modification to a tool or machine is either approved by the manufacturer or is within the design limits of the tool.
14. Before adding any accessory to a tool or machine, be certain that it is both acceptable and safe.
15. Check with your insurance company on policy coverage relating to accidents and other workshop situations.
16. Keep emergency telephone numbers near the telephone. If possible, program the telephone so that one-touch dialing will access emergency numbers.
17. Finally, be informed. Read tool manuals, woodworking magazines, and journals and watch manufacturer-sponsored videos. Note how safety guards are used and how other woodworkers use safety equipment. Stay current on laws and other regulations pertaining to safety and hazardous materials, equipment and procedures.

Safety is a legitimate and proper issue for the workshop. Understanding the way we work and the nature of machines and materials is but another safety procedure.

Appendices

Wood Selection

HOW YOU ARE CHARGED FOR LUMBER

Lumber is sold by the board-foot measure. A board foot is equal to a piece 1 inch thick and 12 inches square. If you know the board-foot price, you can find the cost of any size or shape of lumber by using this formula (thickness and width are in inches and length is in feet):

$$\frac{\text{Thickness} \times \text{width} \times \text{length}}{12} = \text{board feet}$$

Thus a 2 × 4-inch piece of lumber that is 12 feet long would contain 8 board feet:

$$\frac{2 \times 4 \times 12}{12} = 8$$

Lumber is always quoted at a specified price per M (thousand) board feet. For example, if it was quoted at $220 per M board feet, it would be charged for at the rate of $.22 per foot ($\frac{\$200}{1000} = \$.22$). Thus the 8 feet from the formula above would be multiplied times $.22 for a cost of $1.76. The number of board feet in lumber of various sizes and lengths is given in the lumber calculator table on the next page.

It must be remembered, however, that prices are based on *nominal* or original rough sizes rather than *actual* dimensions as sold. In the case of softwoods, the actual thickness and width depend upon whether the pieces are rough-sawn or planed smooth, green or dry. For instance, a green, rough-sawn board 1 inch thick is actually ¾ inch thick if dry and dressed; it is ²⁵⁄₃₂ inch thick if it is green (above 19-percent moisture content) and dressed. If the lumber is grade-marked, the stamp will indicate whether the piece was green or dry when it was dressed to size.

In softwoods, thickness less than 1 inch is charged as a full inch, though in hardwoods the prices vary. The amount of size reduction of hardwoods depends partly on the standards used by the planing mill and partly on the amount of finishing (also called "dressing"). A piece may be dressed on one side only (S1S) or on both sides (S2S) and/or on one edge (S1E) or both edges (S2E). In the accompanying table, it should be kept in mind that the widths of hardwoods vary with various grades.

Lumber is also worked or *milled* to produce popular moulded shapes for specific purposes, such as for baseboards, dowelling, etc. Milled lumber also is dimensioned, but the dimensions may or may not refer to thickness and width. Each shape is dimensioned in a manner necessitated by its usage. When buying milled pieces, you must learn, in each case, what the dealer's dimensions specify (usually, but not always, obvious). Milled lumber is always sold by the *lineal foot* or the piece, based on its length. A lineal-foot measurement, of course, refers to the real length of a board, measured in feet.

LUMBER CALCULATOR

Size in inches	8-foot	10-foot	12-foot	14-foot	16-foot
1 × 2	1⅓	1⅔	2	2⅓	2⅔
1 × 3	2	2½	3	3½	4
1 × 4	2⅔	3⅓	4	4⅔	5⅓
1 × 5	3⅓	4⅙	5	5⅚	6⅔
1 × 6	4	5	6	7	8
1 × 8	5⅓	6⅔	8	9⅓	10⅔
1 × 10	6⅔	8½	10	11⅔	13⅓
1 × 12	8	10	12	14	16
1¼ × 4	3⅓	4⅙	5	5⅚	6⅔
1¼ × 6	5	6¼	7½	8¾	10
1¼ × 8	6⅔	8⅓	10	11⅔	13⅓
1¼ × 10	8⅓	10⁵⁄₁₂	12½	14⁷⁄₁₂	16⅔
1¼ × 12	10	12½	15	17½	20
2 × 4	5⅓	6⅔	8	9⅓	10⅔
2 × 6	8	10	12	14	16
2 × 8	10⅔	13⅓	16	18⅔	21⅓
2 × 10	13⅓	16⅔	20	23⅓	26⅔
2 × 12	16	20	24	28	32
4 × 4	10⅔	13⅓	16	18⅔	21⅓
4 × 6	16	20	24	28	32
4 × 8	21⅓	26⅔	32	37½	42⅔
4 × 10	26⅔	33⅓	40	46⅔	53⅓
4 × 12	32	40	48	56	64
6 × 6	24	30	36	42	48
6 × 8	32	40	48	56	64

NOMINAL AND ACTUAL SIZES OF HARDWOODS

Nominal (rough) size	Surfaced 1 Side (S1S)	Surfaced 2 Sides (S2S)
⅜″	¼″	³⁄₁₆″
½″	⅜″	⁵⁄₁₆″
⅝″	½″	⁷⁄₁₆″
¾″	⅝″	⁹⁄₁₆″
1″	⅞″	1¹³⁄₁₆″
1¼″	1⅛″	1¹⁄₁₆″
1½″	1⅜″	1⁵⁄₁₆″
2″	1¹³⁄₁₆″	1¾″
3″	2¹³⁄₁₆″	2¾″
4″	3¹³⁄₁₆″	3¾″

NOMINAL AND ACTUAL SIZES OF SOFTWOODS

Nominal (rough) size*	THICKNESSES Actual (inches)		Nominal (rough) size*	FACE WIDTHS Actual (inches)	
	Minimum dry**	Dressed green		Minimum dry**	Dressed green
1	¾	25/32	2	1½	1⁹/₁₆
1¼	1	1¹/₃₂	3	2½	2⁹/₁₆
1½	1¼	1⁹/₃₂	4	3½	3⁹/₁₆
2	1½	1⁹/₁₆	6	5½	5⅝
3	2½	2⁹/₁₆	8	7¼	7½
4	3½	3⁹/₁₆	10	9¼	9½
			12	11¼	11½

* Thickness sometimes is expressed as 4/4, 5/4, etc.

** Dry lumber has been seasoned to a moisture content of 19 percent or less.

HOW WOOD IS GRADED

When a lumber dealer refers to "boards," he means stock less than 2 inches thick and usually more than 6 inches wide. Narrower boards are "strips."

Dimension lumber, also called *framing* lumber, includes structural pieces from 2 to 5 inches thick, used for studs, joists, and rafters. Lumber 5 inches thick or more is *timber.*

Each type is sold in various grades according to the size, number, and kind of defects found in them. Softwoods and hardwoods are graded differently; there is no relation between softwood and hardwood grades.

SOFTWOOD LUMBER GRADES

SELECT

(Lumber of good appearance and finishing qualities)

Suitable for Natural Finishes

GRADE A (also called No. 1 Clear). Free of defects. Because of cost, this grade is not stocked in all lumberyards.

GRADE B (also called No. 2 Clear). Allows a few small defects and blemishes. (A slightly higher category—B & Better—is sold by lumberyards. While not an "official" grade, it contains a few pieces of Grade A, but the majority is Grade B. This is slightly more expensive than Grade B itself.)

Suitable for Paint Finishes

GRADE C. Allows a limited number of small defects or blemishes that can be covered with paint. Some pieces can even take a natural finish.

GRADE D. Allows any number of defects or blemishes that do not detract from a finish appearance, especially when painted.

COMMON

(Lumber containing defects or blemishes which detract from a finish appearance, but which is suitable for general utility and construction use.)

Lumber Suitable for Use Without Waste

NO. 1 COMMON (also called Construction Grade). Good, sound, watertight lumber with tight knots (none larger than 2 inches and rarely on edges) and limited blemishes. No warp, splits, checks, or decay.

NO. 2 COMMON (also called Standard Grade). Allows larger and coarser defects than No. 1, but is considered grain-tight lumber.

Lumber Permitting Waste

NO. 3 COMMON (also called Utility Grade). Allows larger and coarser defects than No. 2 and occasional knotholes.

NO. 4 COMMON (also called Economy Grade). Low-quality lumber admitting the coarsest defects, such as decay and knotholes.

NO. 5 COMMON. Practically waste lumber, good only for use as a filler, and then with considerable waste.

HARDWOOD LUMBER GRADES

Hardwood grading is not consistent for all trees, nor in all parts of the country. On the whole, however, the grades are as follows:

FIRSTS: Lumber that is $91\frac{2}{3}$-percent clear on both sides; considered the best possible for cabinetwork.

SECONDS: Lumber that is $83\frac{1}{3}$-percent clear on both sides; still very good for most cabinetwork.

FIRSTS & SECONDS: A selection that must contain not less than 20-percent firsts.

SELECTS (in alder, ash, beech, birch, cherry, chestnut, mahogany, maple, sycamore, and walnut only): Lumber that is 90-percent clear on one side only (other side not graded). Good for most cabinetwork, with some waste.

SAPS (in poplar only): Approximately the same as select above.

NO. 1 COMMON: One side only, $66\frac{2}{3}$-percent clear. With waste, good for interior and less demanding cabinetwork.

NO. 2 COMMON: One side only, 50-percent clear. Okay for painting, some panelling and flooring.

STAINED SAPS (in poplar only): Equivalent to No. 2 common, above.

NO. 3A COMMON: One side only, $33\frac{1}{3}$-percent clear.

NO. 3B COMMON: One side only, 25-percent clear.

SOUND-WORMY (in chestnut only): A No. 1 above but with wormholes.

Notes: Hardwoods are supposed to be free of warp, wind, bad splits, and checks. "Clear" refers to the number of clear cuttings that can be obtained.

COMMON HOME WORKSHOP WOODS

Name of Wood	Hardness	Strength	Stability	Weight	Rot resistance	Split resistance	Working quality for hand tools	Shaping	Turning	Mortising	Planing and jointing	Nailing	Gluing	Sanding	Cost
Alder	medium	weak	G	light	F	F	G	F	F	F	G	G	G	F	medium
Ash, white	medium	medium	E	medium heavy	F	G	P	E	F	F	G	G	F	E	medium
Balsa	soft	weak	G	light	P	E	E	P	P	P	G	E	E	P	low
Basswood	soft	weak	G	light	P	E	E	P	P	F	G	E	E	P	medium
Beech	hard	medium	P	heavy	P	G	F	F	F	G	F	P	G	G	medium
Birch	hard	strong	G	heavy	P	G	P	E	G	E	G	P	F	F	high
Butternut	soft	weak	E	light	F	F	G	F	G	F	G	F	G	F	medium
Cedar, red	soft	weak	G	medium	E	P	G	P	P	F	F	P	G	P	medium
Cherry	medium	medium	G	heavy	F	P	G	E	E	E	E	F	E	E	high
Chestnut	soft	weak	E	light	E	P	G	G	E	G	G	G	E	E	high
Cottonwood	soft	weak	G	light	P	E	E	P	P	P	G	E	E	P	low
Cypress	soft	medium	G	light	E	F	F	P	P	P	G	F	F	F	medium
Elm	medium	medium	P	medium heavy	F	G	F	P	P	G	P	E	F	G	medium
Fir, Douglas	medium	medium strong	F	medium heavy	G	F	F	P	P	G	G	G	G	F	medium
Fir, white		low		light	G	G	G	P	P	G	G	G	G	G	low
Gum, red	medium	medium	P	medium	F	G	G	F	E	F	F	G	E	F	medium
Hickory	hard	strong	G	heavy	P	F	P	F	G	E	G	P	G	E	medium
Lauan	medium	medium	E	medium	G	P	G	F	G	F	G	G	E	P	medium
Magnolia	soft	weak	F	medium	F	G	G	G	F	P	G	E	E	G	medium
Mahogany	medium	medium	E	medium heavy	F	P	G	E	E	E	G	G	E	G	high
Maple, hard	hard	strong	G	heavy	P	P	P	E	E	E	F	P	F	G	high
Maple, soft	medium	medium	F	medium	F	G	G	F	F	P	P	F	G	G	medium
Oak, red	hard	strong	E	heavy	P	F	P	F	G	E	E	G	E	E	medium
Oak, white	hard	strong	E	heavy	F	F	P	G	G	E	E	G	G	E	high
Pine, ponderosa	soft	weak	G	light	F	P	E	G	G	F	G	E	E	F	low
Pine, sugar	soft	weak	G	light	F	P	E	G	G	F	G	E	E	P	low
Pine, white	soft	weak	G	light	F	P	E	G	G	F	G	E	E	G	low
Pine, yellow	hard	strong	F	heavy	G	P	F	G	P	G	G	F	F	F	medium
Poplar	soft	weak	G	medium	P	G	E	P	G	F	G	E	E	P	medium
Redwood	soft	medium	E	medium	E	G	G	G	F	P	G	G	E	P	medium
Spruce	soft	weak	G	light	F	F	G	G	G	F	G	G	G	G	medium
Sycamore	medium	medium	P	heavy	F	G	G	P	G	E	P	E	G	P	medium
Walnut	medium	strong	E	heavy	G	F	G	G	E	E	G	F	E	E	high
Willow	soft	weak	G	light	G	G	G	F	F	F	F	G	G	G	low

(E = Excellent, G = Good, F = Fair, P = Poor)

COMMON GRADES OF PLYWOOD

EXTERIOR

Grade (exterior)	Face	Back	Inner plies	Uses
A-A	A	A	C	Outdoors, where appearance of both sides is important
A-B	A	B	C	Alternate for A-A, where appearance of one side is less important; face is finish grade
A-C	A	C	C	Soffits, fences, base for coatings
B-C	B	C	C	For utility uses such as farm buildings, some kinds of fences, etc., base for coatings
303 Siding	C (or better)	C	C	Panels with variety of surface texture and grooving patterns; for siding, fences, panelling, screens, etc.
T1-11	C	C	C	Special ⅝-inch siding panel with deep parallel grooves; available unsanded, textured, or MDO surface
C-C (plugged)	C (plugged)	C	C	Excellent base for tile and linoleum, backing for wall coverings, high-performance coatings
C-C	C	C	C	Unsanded, for backing and rough construction exposed to weather
B-B Plyform	B	B	C	Concrete forms; reuse until wood literally wears out
MDO	B	B or C	C	Medium Density Overlay—ideal base for paint; for siding, built-ins, signs, displays
HDO	A or B	A or B	C-plugged or C	High Density Overlay—hard surface; no paint needed; for concrete forms, cabinets, counter tops, tanks

COMMON GRADES OF PLYWOOD

INTERIOR

Grade (interior)	Face	Back	Inner plies	Uses
A-A	A	A	D	Cabinet doors, built-ins, furniture where both sides will show
A-B	A	B	D	Alternate of A-A, face is finish grade, back is solid and smooth
A-D	A	D	D	Finish-grade face for panelling, built-ins, backing
B-D	B	D	D	Utility grade; for backing, cabinet sides, etc.
C-D	C	D	D	Sheathing and structural uses such as temporary enclosures, subfloor; unsanded
Underlayment	C-plugged	D	C[1] and D	For separate underlayment under tile, carpeting
Sturd-I-Floor	C-plugged	D	C[1] and D	For combination subfloor-underlayment under tile, carpeting

ELECTRICITY CONSUMPTION: APPLIANCES

	Watts
Air conditioner, room	800 to 1500
Blanket	150 to 200
Blender	250 to 300
Broiler	1200 to 1600
Can opener	80 to 120
Coffeemaker	600 to 1000
Deep fryer	1200 to 1650
Dishwasher	600 to 1300
Dryer, clothes	4000 to 8700
Fan, portable	50 to 200
Food mixer	120 to 250
Freezer, home	300 to 500
Frying pan	1000 to 1300
Furnace blower	800
Garbage disposal unit	200 to 800
Grill	1000 to 1200
Heat lamp	250
Heater, portable, home	600 to 1650
Heater, portable, home, 230-volt	2800 to 5600
Heating pad	50 to 75
Hot plate, each burner	550 to 1200
Iron, hand	660 to 1500
Ironer	1200 to 1650
Lamps, fluorescent	15 to 60
Lamps, incandescent	2 up
Microwave oven	800 to 1500
Motors: 1/4 horsepower	300 to 400
1/2 horsepower	450 to 600
1 horsepower	950 to 1000
Radio, transistor	6 to 12
Radio, tube	35 to 150
Range, oven and all burners	8000 to 16000
Refrigerator	150 to 300
Roaster	1200 to 1650
Rotisserie-broiler	1200 to 1650
Sewing machine	60 to 90
Shaver	8 to 12
Stereo	100 to 400
Television	200 to 400
Toaster	550 to 1200
Trash compactor	300 to 500
Vacuum cleaner	200 to 800
Waffle iron	600 to 1100
Washing machine	400 to 800
Water heater	2000 to 5000
Water pump	300 to 700

COPPER WIRE TABLE
(Brown & Sharpe or American Wire Gauge)

AWG B&S	Diameter in mills	Turns per linear inch		Feet per pound		Ohms per 1000 feet at 68° F
		Enamel	Double cotton covered	Bare	Double cotton covered	
1	289.3	—	—	3.947	—	.1264
2	257.6	—	—	4.977	—	.1593
3	229.4	—	—	6.276	—	.2009
4	204.3	—	—	7.914	—	.2533
5	181.9	—	—	9.980	—	.3195
6	162.0	—	—	12.58	—	.4028
7	144.3	—	—	15.87	—	.5080
8	128.5	7.6	7.1	20.01	19.6	.6405
9	114.4	8.6	7.8	25.23	24.6	.8077
10	101.9	9.6	8.9	31.82	30.9	1.018
11	90.74	10.7	9.8	40.12	38.8	1.284
12	80.81	12.0	10.9	50.59	48.9	1.619
13	71.96	13.5	12.0	63.80	61.5	2.042
14	64.08	15.0	13.8	80.44	77.3	2.575
15	57.07	16.8	14.7	101.4	97.3	3.247
16	50.82	18.9	16.4	127.9	119	4.094
17	45.26	21.2	18.1	161.3	150	5.163
18	40.30	23.6	19.8	203.4	188	6.510
19	35.89	26.4	21.8	256.5	237	8.210
20	31.96	29.4	23.8	323.4	298	10.35
21	28.46	33.1	26.0	407.8	370	13.05
22	25.35	37.0	30.0	514.2	461	16.46
23	22.57	41.3	31.6	648.5	584	20.76
24	20.10	46.3	35.6	817.7	745	26.17
25	17.90	51.7	38.6	1031	903	33.00
26	15.94	58.0	41.8	1300	1118	41.62
27	14.20	64.9	45.0	1639	1422	52.48
28	12.64	72.7	48.5	2067	1759	66.17
29	11.26	81.6	51.8	2607	2207	83.44
30	10.03	90.5	55.5	3287	2534	105.2
31	8.928	101	59.2	4145	2768	132.7
32	7.950	113	62.6	5227	3137	167.3
33	7.080	127	66.3	6591	4697	211.0
34	6.305	143	70.0	8310	6168	266.0
35	5.615	158	73.5	10480	6737	335.0
36	5.000	.175	77.0	13210	7877	423.0
37	4.453	198	80.3	16660	9309	533.4
38	3.965	224	83.6	21010	10666	672.6
39	3.531	248	86.6	26500	11907	848.1
40	3.145	282	89.7	33410	14222	1069

A mil is 1/1000 (one-thousandth) of an inch.

Measurements of covered wires may vary slightly with different manufacturers.

Wire of size 6 and larger is always stranded. The diameters shown here, however, are those of solid wires of equivalent cross section.

What Size Wire for the Circuit?

The minimum-size wire to be used in electrical circuits is determined by both safety and efficiency. In all cases, wiring installations should conform to the rules of the National Electrical Code, which is based on the recommendations of the National Fire Protection Association. This code is concerned only with preventing electrical or thermal hazards that might electrocute somebody or start a fire. Beyond the bare requirements of safety, however, circuits should be designed to not waste too much electricity in the form of useless heat so that they deliver current at the end of the line at a sufficiently high voltage to properly do the job.

WIRE GAUGES FOR FEEDER AND BRANCH CIRCUITS*

Amperes	Continuous operation		Noncontinuous operation	
	Wire size (copper)	Wire size (aluminum)	Wire size (copper)	Wire size (aluminum)
15	14	12	14	12
20	12	10	12	10
25/30	10	8	10	8
35/40	8	6	8	6
45/50	6	4	6	4
60	4	4	4	4
70	4	3	4	3
80	3	2	3	3
90	2	1	3	2
100	1	0	2	1
110	0	00	1	0
125	0	000	1	00
150	00	0000	0	000
175	000		00	0000
200	0000		000	
225			0000	

* American Wire Gauge (AWG) sizes. Continuous loads are those expected to continue for 3 or more hours; noncontinuous loads are those where 67 percent or less of the load is expected to be continuous.

RESISTANCE OF COPPER WIRE

In estimating the resistance of copper wire, it may help to remember several approximate relationships:

Size wire AWG, B&S	Ohms per 1,000 feet	Feet per ohm
10	1	1,000
20	10	100
30	100	10
40	1,000	1

An increase of 1 in AWG or B&S wire size increases resistance 25 percent.
An increase of 2 increases resistance 60 percent.
An increase of 3 increases resistance 100 percent.

WIRING-SIZE DATA (ENCLOSED WIRES)

Wire size	Maximum ampere rating	
	Types R, RW, RU, T, and TW	Types RH and RHW
14	15	15
12	20	20
10	30	30
8	40	45
6	55	65
4	70	85
3	80	100
2	95	115
1	110	130
0	125	150
00	145	175
000	165	200

CONDUIT SIZE AND AMPERE CAPACITY OF WIRES IN CONDUIT

Number of wires (1 to 9) to be installed in conduit (exact number will vary according to local code)

Wire size	Ampere capacity	½-inch conduit	¾-inch conduit	1-inch conduit	1¼-inch conduit
14	15	4	6	9	9
12	20	3	5	8	9
10	25	1	4	7	9
8	35	1	3	4	7
6	45	1	1	3	4
4	60	1	1	1	3
5	95	1	1	1	3

Extension Cords

The 125-volt all-purpose extension cords for indoor or outdoor use are generally marked type "SJT." Two conductor cords are okay for double-insulated tools with a two-prong plug, but tools with three-prong grounded plugs must be used only with three-wire grounded extension cords connected to properly grounded three-wire receptacles. Current National Electrical Code specs call for outdoor receptacles to be protected with ground-fault detector devices.

When you buy a new extension cord, check the table below or the maker's specs and permanently mark or tag it for capacity. For example, mark a 50-foot cord "13A" to indicate it's good for a maximum 13-ampere load.

HOW TO SELECT THE PROPER EXTENSION CORD

Cord length	0-5A	6A	7A	8A	9A	10A	11A	12A	13A	14A	15A	16A	17A	18A	19A	20A
						Ampere rating for 110–120 V.A.C. tools										
25 feet	18	18	18	18	18	18	16	16	16	14	14	14	14	14	12	12
50 feet	18	18	18	18	18	18	16	16	16	14	14	14	14	14	12	12
75 feet	18	18	18	18	16	16	16	16	16	14	14	14	14	14	12	12
100 feet	18	16	16	16	16	16	16	16	14	14	14	14	14	14	12	12
125 feet	16	16	16	16	16	14	14	14	14	14	14	12	12	12	12	12
150 feet	16	16	14	14	14	14	14	14	14	12	12	12	12	12	12	12

* Wire sizes are AWG (American Wire Gauge); recommendations are minimum allowable. For nameplate ampere ratings that fall between those given here, use the extension cord recommended for the next higher ampere. If the tool has a long supply cord, this should be added when figuring total extension cord length.

REQUIRED CONDUCTOR INSULATION
FOR CURRENT-CARRYING CIRCUITS UNDER 6,000 VOLTS

Trade name	Type letter	Insulation	Outer covering	Use
Code	R	code-grade rubber	moisture-resistant, flame-retardant fibrous covering	general use
Moisture resistant	RW	moisture-resistant rubber	moisture-resistant, flame-retardant fibrous covering	general use, especially in wet locations
Heat resistant	RH	heat-resistant rubber	moisture-resistant, flame-retardant fibrous covering	general use
Latex rubber	RU	90-percent unmilled grainless rubber	moisture-resistant, flame-retardant fibrous covering	general use
Thermoplastic	T and TW	flame-retardant thermoplastic compound	none	T—general use TW—in wet locations
Thermoplastic and asbestos	TA	thermoplastic and asbestos	flame-retardant cotton braid	switchboard wiring only
Asbestos and varnished cambric	AVA	impregnated asbestos and varnished cambric	asbestos braid	dry location only
Asbestos and varnished cambric	AVB	same as type AVA	flame-retardant cotton braid	dry location only
Asbestos and varnished cambric	AVL	same as type AVA	asbestos braid and lead sheath	wet location
Slow-burning	SB	three braids of impregnated fire-retardant cotton thread	outer cover finished smooth and hard	dry locations only
Slow-burning weatherproof	SBW	two layers of impregnated cotton thread	outer fire-retardant coating	open wiring only

Appliance Grounding

The one electrical problem most often overlooked is improper or inadequate grounding or none at all. It has been estimated by the Injury Control Program of the National Center for Urban and Industrial Health that there are 500,000 household injuries each year as the direct result of accidents with major and portable electrical appliances used in the home. The U.S. Bureau of Vital Statistics lists over 1,000 deaths each year due to electric shock. Proper grounding would have eliminated many of these injuries and deaths.

It has been determined that electric current (amperage), not voltage, is the dangerous ingredient of electricity. Measurements of a 60-Hz, 120-V current and the predicted body reaction are given in the accompanying table:

Current	Effect
0.05 to 2 mA (5/10,000 to 2/1,000A)	Just noticeable
2 to 10 mA (2/1,000 to 10/1,000A)	Slight to strong muscular reaction
5 to 25 mA (5/1,000 to 25/1,000A)	Strong shock, inability to let go
25 to 50 mA (25/1,000 to 50/1,000A)	Violent muscular contraction
50 to 200 mA (50/1,000 to 200/1,000A)	Irregular twitching of the heart muscles with no pumping action (ventricular fibrillation)
100 mA and over (100/1,000A)	Paralysis of breathing

A person's skin, when dry, may have from 100,000 to as high as 600,000 ohms resistance; however, when the skin is wet (such as when perspiring), resistance can drop below 1,000 ohms. Let us assume a technician is working on a 120-V motor with an insulation break leaking current to an ungrounded motor frame. Ohm's Law (volts/ohms = amperes) may be used to compute the amount of current received by the technician's body. If his skin is dry, the current would be 120 V/100,000 ohms = 0.0012A, or 1.2 mA. This current would be barely noticeable. However, if the technician is perspiring, his skin resistance may be 1,000 ohms or less (with a break in the skin it can be as low as 200 ohms). Using Ohm's Law, the current would be 0.12A, or 120 mA (120 V/1,000 ohms = 0.12A). This is more than a lethal current. If the motor frame had been grounded, this leaking current would have bled to the ground, and the fuse or breaker would generally have "blown." Remember, as little as 0.025A at 120 V can kill.

WATTAGE FOR HOME LIGHTING

Room	General area lighting		Local lighting		Remarks
	Bulb	Fluorescent	Bulb	Fluorescent	
Living, dining room	150	60–80	40–150	15–40	For small living rooms
Bedroom	200		40–100		Average size
Bath	100–150	80	Two 60s	Two 20s	Task lights on both sides of mirror
Kitchen	150–200	60–80	60	10 per foot of counter	Fixture over eating area or sink—150 watt bulb, 60-watt fluorescent
Halls, service	75	32			Plus low-wattage night lights
Hall entrance	100	60			
Stairway	75	32			Shielded fixtures at top and bottom controlled by three-way switch
Outdoors, entry and access	40				Wall brackets aimed down
Hall entrance	100	60			
Outdoors, yard	100–150 projector				Controlled from garage and house
Laundry	Two 150s	Two 80s			Placed over washing and ironing areas
Workshop	150	80	60	10 per foot of bench	Task lights aimed at machines
Garage	Two 100s				On ceiling, center of each side of car

CONVERSIONS OF COMMON UNITS

To convert from	To	Multiply by
Acceleration by gravity	centimetres per second	980.665
	feet per second	32.16
Acres	hectares	0.4047
	square chains	10.0
	square feet	43,560.0
	square miles	0.00156
	centiares	100.0
	square yards	119.6
Atmospheres (atm)	inches of mercury	29.921
	feet of water	33.934
	kilograms per square centimetre	1.033228
	pounds per square inch	14.6959
British thermal units (Btu)	calories	0.252
	foot-pounds	778.0
	watt-seconds	1,054.86
Bushels	bushels, imperial	0.968
	cubic feet	1.2445
	cubic inches	2,150.42
	litres	35.2393
	pecks	4.0
	pints, dry	64.0
	quarts, dry	32.0
Calories (cal)	British thermal units	3.9682
	foot-pounds	3,088.4
Candles per square centimetre	Lamberts	3.142
Candles per square inch	Lamberts	0.4869
Carats	grains	3.086
Centares	square inches	1,549.997
	square metres	1.0
Centigrade, degrees (°C)	Fahrenheit, degrees	$\frac{9}{5} \times °C + 32$
Centigrams (cg)	grains	0.1543
	grams	0.01
Centilitres (cl)	litres	0.01
	ounces; fluid	0.0338
Centimetres (cm)	feet	0.0328
	inches	0.3937
	metres	0.01

To convert from	To	Multiply by
Chains (surveyor's)	furlongs	0.10000
	miles, statute	0.01250
	links	100.0
Circle (angular)	degrees	360.0
Circular inch (cir in)	area of a 1-inch- diametre circle	1.0
	circular mils	1,000,000.0
	square inches	0.7854
Circular mil	area of a 0.001-inch diametre circle	1.0
	circular inches	0.0000001
Circumference of the earth at the equator	miles, nautical	21,600.0
Circumference of the earth at the equator	miles, statute	24,874.5
Cord (cd), of wood, (4 × 4 × 8)	cubic feet	128.0
Cubic centimetres (cu cm)	cubic feet	0.00003531
	cubic inches	0.06102
Cubic centimetres (cu cm)	litres	0.0010
	cubic metre	0.0000010
Cubic decimetres	cubic centimetres	1,000.0
	cubic inches	61.02
Cubic feet (cu ft)	bushels	0.80290
	cords, of wood	0.00781
	cubic centimetres	28,317.08
	cubic inches	1,728.0
	cubic metres	0.0283
	cubic yards	0.0370
	gallons	7.4805
	litres	28.3163
	perch, of masonry	0.04040
Cubic feet of water at 39.1° Fahrenheit (°F)	kilograms	28.3156
	pounds	62.4245
Cubic inches (cu in)	bushels, imperial	0.00045
	bushels	0.00046
	cubic centimetres	16.3872
	cubic feet	0.00058
	cubic metres	0.000016
	cubic yards	0.0000214
	gallons	0.00432
	litres	0.0164

CONVERSIONS OF COMMON UNITS *(Continued)*

To convert from	To	Multiply by
	pecks	0.00186
	pints, dry	0.02976
	pints, liquid	0.0346
	quarts, dry	0.01488
	quarts, liquid	0.0173
Cubic metres (cu m or m³)	cubic centimetres	1,000,000.0
	cubic feet	35.3133
	cubic inches	61,023.3753
	cubic yards	1.3079
	gallons	264.170
Cubic millimetres (cu mm or mm³)	cubic centimetres	0.001
	cubic inches	0.00006
Cubic yards (cu yd)	cubic feet	27.0
	cubic inches	46,656.0
	cubic metres	0.7646
Decagrams	grams	10.0
	ounces, avoirdupois	0.3527
Decilitres	bushels	0.284
	gallons	2.64
	litres	10.0
Decametres	inches	393.7
	metres	10.0
Decigrams	grains	1.5432
	grams	0.1
Decilitre	ounces, fluid	0.338
Decilitres	litres	0.1
Decimetres	inches	3.937
	metres	0.01
Degrees (arc)	radians	0.0175
Degrees (at the equator)	miles, nautical	60.0
	miles, statute	69.168
Degrees (deg or °)	minutes	60.0
Dozens (doz)	units	12.0
Drams (dr), apothecaries'	grains	60.0
	grams	3.543
	scruples	3.0

To convert from	To	Multiply by
Drams, avoirdupois	grains	27.344
	grams	1.772
	ounces, avoirdupois	0.0625
Drams, fluid	cubic inches	0.2256
	millilitres	3.6966
Drams, fluid	minims	60.0
	ounces, fluid	0.125
Dynes	grams	0.00102
Fahrenheit	centigrade, degrees	$\dfrac{5(°F-32)}{9}$
Fathoms	feet	6.0
	metres	1.8288
	yards	2.0
Feet (ft)	centimetres	30.4801
	fathom	0.16667
	inches	12.0
	links	0.66000
	metres	0.3048
	miles	0.000189
	miles, nautical	0.0001645
	rods	0.06061
	yards	0.3333
Feet of water at 62° Fahrenheit	killigrams per square metre	304.442
	pounds per square foot	62.355
	pounds per square inch	0.4334
Feet per second (fps)	knots	0.5921
	miles per hour	0.6816
Foot-pounds (ft-lb)	British thermal units	0.00129
	calories	0.00032
	metre-kilograms	0.13835
Foot-pounds per minute	horsepower	0.000003
Foot-pounds per second	horsepower	0.000018
Furlongs	chains	10.0
	feet	660.0
	metres	201.17
	miles, statute	0.12500
	yards	220.0
Gallons (gal)	ounces, U.S. fluid	128.0
Gallons, imperial	gallons, U.S.	1.2009

CONVERSIONS OF COMMON UNITS *(Continued)*

To convert from	To	Multiply by
Gallons (gal), imperial	litres	4.54607
Gallons, U.S.	cubic feet	0.1337
	cubic inches	231.0
	cubic metres	0.0038
	gallons, imperial	0.8327
	litres	3.7878
Gallons, U.S., water	pounds	8.5
Gills	pints, liquid	0.25
Grains	drams, avoirdupois	0.0366
	grams	0.0648
	milligrams	64.7989
	ounces, avoirdupois	0.00229
	ounces, troy and apothecaries'	0.00208
	pounds, avoirdupois	0.00014
	pounds, troy and apothecaries'	0.00017
Grams (g)	dynes	981.0
	grains	15.4475
	kilograms	0.0010
	milligrams	1,000.0
	ounces, avoirdupois	0.0353
	pounds, avoirdupois	0.0022
Grams per cubic centimetre	kilograms per cubic metre	1,000.0
	pounds per cubic foot	62.4
	pounds per cubic inch	0.03613
Gross	dozen	12.0
Gross, great	gross	12.0
Hands	inches	4.0
Hectares	square metres	10,000.0
	acres	2.471
Hectograms	grams	100.0
	ounces, avoirdupois	3.5274
Hectolitres	gallons	26.417
	litres	100.0
Hectometres	feet	328.083
	metres	100.0

To convert from	To	Multiply by
Horsepower (hp)	kilogram-metres per second	76.042
	foot-pounds per second	550.0
	foot-pounds per minute	33,000.0
	metric horsepower	1.0139
	watts per minute	746.0
Horsepower, metric	horsepower	0.9862
	foot pounds per minute	32,550.0
	foot pounds per second	542.5
	kilogram-metres per second	75.0
Inches (in)	centimetres	2.5400
	feet	0.08333
	hands	0.25000
	links	0.12626
	metres	0.0254
	mils	1,000.0
	spans	0.11111
	yards	0.02778
Inches of mercury	feet of water	1.1341
	grams per square centimetre	34.542
	inches of water	13.6092
	pounds per square inch	0.49115
Inches of water	grams per square centimetre	2.537
	inches of mercury	0.07347
	pounds per square foot	5.1052
Kilocycles	cycles per second	1,000.0
Kilogram-metres (kg-m)	pound-feet	7.2330
Kilogram-metres per second	horsepower	0.01305
	horsepower, metric	0.01333
Kilograms (kg)	grains	15,432.36
	grams	1,000.0
	ounces, avoirdupois	35.2740
	pounds, avoirdupois	2.2046
	tons	0.00110
	tons, long	0.00098
	tons, metric	0.001
Kilograms per cubic metre (kg per cu m or kg/m³)	pounds per cubic foot	0.06243
Kilograms per metre	pounds per foot	0.6721
Kilograms per square centimetre	pounds per square inch	14.22

CONVERSIONS OF COMMON UNITS *(Continued)*

To convert from	To	Multiply by
Kilograms per square metre	pounds per square inch	0.2048
	pounds per square inch	0.00142
Kilolitres (kl)	litres	1,000.0
Kilometres (km)	feet	3,280.8330
	metres	1,000.0
	miles, nautical	0.5396
	miles, statute	0.6214
Kilometres per hour	knots	0.5396
	miles per hour	0.62138
Kilowatt-hours (kwhr)	British thermal units per hour	3,412.75
	horsepower hours	1.3414
Kilowatts (kw)	foot-pounds per minute	0.04426
Knots	feet per second	1.6889
	kilometres per hour	1.8532
	metres per second	0.5148
	miles per hour	1.1516
	nautical miles per hour	1.0
Lamberts	candles per square centimetre	0.3183
	candles per square inch	2.054
Leagues, land	kilometres	4.83
	miles, nautical	2.6050
	miles, statute	3.0
Leagues, marine	kilometres	5.56
	miles, nautical	3.0
	miles, statute	3.45
Links	chains	0.01
	feet	0.66
	inches	7.92
	rods	0.04
	yards	0.22
Litres (l)	cubic centimetres	1,000.0
	cubic feet	0.035313
	cubic inches	61.02398
	gallons, imperial	0.2199
	gallons, U.S.	0.2641
	pecks	0.1135
	quarts, dry	0.9081
	quarts, liquid	1.0567

To convert from	To	Multiply by
Long tons	pounds, avoirdupois	2,240.0
Lumens per square foot	foot-candles	1.0
Lux	foot-candles	0.0929
Megacycles	cycles per second	1,000,000.0
Megametres	metres	100,000.0
Metre-kilograms (m-kg)	foot-pounds	7.2330
Metres (m)	fathoms	0.5468
	feet	3.2808
	inches	39.370
	miles, nautical	0.000541
Metres (m)	miles	0.000622
	yards	1.0936
Metres per second	knots	1.9425
	miles per hour	2.2369
Microns	inches	0.000039
	metres	0.000001
	mils	0.03937
Miles, nautical	feet	6,080.20
	kilometres	1.85325
	leagues, marine	0.33333
	metres	1,853.2486
	miles, statute	1.1516
Miles per hour (mph)	feet per second	1.4667
	kilometres per hour	1.6093
	knots	0.8684
	metres per second	0.4470
Miles, statute	chains	80.0
	feet	5,280.0
	furlongs	8.0
	kilometres	1.6093
	leagues, land	0.33333
	metres	1,609.35
	miles, nautical	0.86836
	yards	1,760.0
Milligrams (mg)	grains	0.01543
	grams	0.001
Millilitres (ml)	drams, fluid	0.2705
	litres	0.001
	ounces, fluid	0.0338

CONVERSIONS OF COMMON UNITS *(Continued)*

To convert from	To	Multiply by
Millimetres (mm)	inches	0.03937
	metres	0.001
	microns	1,000.0
	mils	39.37
Mils	inches	0.001
	microns	25.4001
	millimetres	0.0254
Minims	drams, fluid	0.01667
Minutes (min)	seconds	60.0
Myriagrams	grams	10,000.0
Myriametres	metres	10,000.0
Ounces (oz), apothecaries'	drams, apothecaries'	8.0
Ounces, avoirdupois	drams, avoirdupois	16.0
	grains	437.5
	grams	28.3495
	ounces, troy and apothecaries'	1.0971
	pounds, avoirdupois	0.0625
Ounces, British fluid	cubic centimetres	28.382
	cubic inches	1.732
Ounces, fluid	millimetres	29.57
Ounces, troy	pennyweights	20.0
Ounces, troy and apothecaries'	grains	480.0
	grams	31.10348
	ounces, avoirdupois	0.91149
Ounces, U.S. fluid	cubic inches	1.805
	drams, fluid	8.0
	gallons	0.00781
	litres	0.0296
Pecks (pk)	bushels	0.25
	cubic inches	537.61
	litres	8.8096
	quarts, dry	8.0
Pennyweights (dwt)	grains	24.0
Perch (of masonry)	cubic feet	24.75
Pints (pt), dry	bushels	0.015625
	cubic inches	33.60
	litres	0.5506

To convert from	To	Multiply by
Pints (pt), dry	pecks	0.0625
	quarts, dry	0.5
Pints, liquid	cubic inches	28,875.0
	gills	4.0
	litres	0.4732
Poundals	pounds, avoirdupois	0.03113
Pound-feet (lb-ft)	kilogram-metres	0.1383
Pounds (lb), avoirdupois	cubic feet of water	0.0160
	grains	7,000.0
	grams	453.5924
	ounces, avoirdupois	16.0
	poundals	32.1740
	slugs	0.0311
	tons, long	0.00045
	tons, short	0.0005
Pounds per cubic foot (lb per cu ft)	grams per cubic centimetre	0.01602
	kilograms per cubic metre	16.0184
	pounds per cubic inch	0.00058
Pounds per foot	kilograms per metre	1.4882
Pounds per square foot (psf)	inches of water	0.1922
	kilograms per square metre	4.8824
	pounds per square inch	0.00694
Pounds per square inch (psi)	atmospheres	0.0680
	feet of water	2.3066
	grams per square centimetre	70.3067
	inches of water	27.7
	inches of mercury	2.0360
	kilograms per square metre	703.0669
	pounds per square foot	144.0
Pounds, troy and apothecaries'	grains	5,760.0
	kilograms	0.37324
Pounds, troy and apothecaries'	ounces, troy and apothecaries'	12.0
	pounds, avoirdupois	0.8229
Quadrants	degrees	90.0

CONVERSIONS OF COMMON UNITS *(Continued)*

To convert from	To	Multiply by
Quarts, dry	litres	1.1012
	pecks	0.125
	pints, dry	2.0
	quarts, dry, imperial	0.968
	bushels, U.S.	0.03125
	cubic inches	67.2
Quarts, liquid	cubic inches	57.75
	litres	0.94636
Quintals	grams	100,000.0
	pounds, avoirdupois	220.46
Radians	degrees, arc	57.2958
	minutes, arc	3,437.7468
	revolutions	0.1591
Radians per second	revolutions per minute	9.4460
Ream	sheets	480.0
Ream, printing paper	sheets	500.0
Revolutions	radians	6.2832
Revolutions per minute (rpm)	radians per second	0.1059
Rods	chains	0.25
	feet	16.5
	furlongs	40.0
	links	25.0
	metres	5.029
	yards	5.5
Score	units	20.0
Scruples	grains	20.0
Seconds	minutes	0.01667
Slugs	pounds	32.1740
Spans	inches	9.0
Square centimetres (sq cm or cm²)	square feet	0.001076
	square inches	0.1550
	square millimetres	100.0

To convert from	To	Multiply by
Square chains	acres	0.1
	square feet	4,356.0
	square metres	404.7
	square miles	0.00016
	square rods	16.0
	square yards	484.0
Square decametres	square metres	100.0
Square decimetres	square metres	0.01
Square feet (sq ft)	acres	0.000022988
	square centimetres	929.0341
	square chains	0.00023
	square inches	144.0
	square metres	0.0929
	square rods	0.00368
	square yards	0.11111
Square hectometres	square metres	10,000.0
Square inches (sq in)	circular inches	1.27324
	square centimetres	6.4516
	square feet	0.00694
	square millimetres	645.1625
	square yards	0.00077
Square kilometres (sq km or km²)	hectares	100.0
	square metres	1,000,000.0
	square miles	0.3861
Square links	square feet	0.4356
	square metres	0.0405
	square rods	0.00160
	square yards	0.04840
Square metres (sq m or m²)	centiares	1.0
	square feet	10.7639
	square yards	1.1960
Square miles	square kilometres	2.590
	acres	640.0
	square chains	6,400.0
Square millimetres (sq mm or mm²)	square inches	0.00155
	square metres	0.000001

CONVERSIONS OF COMMON UNITS

To convert from	To	Multiply by
Square rods	square chains	0.06250
	square feet	272.25
	square links	625.0
	square metres	25.29
	square yards	30.25
Square yards	square chains	0.00207
	square feet	9.0
	square inches	1,296.0
	square links	20.66116
	square metres	0.83613
	square rods	0.03306
Tons, long	kilograms	1,016.0470
	pounds, avoirdupois	2,240.0
Tons, metric	kilograms	1,000.0
	pounds, avoirdupois	2,204.62
	quintals	10.0
Tons of refrigeration	BTU per hour	12,000.0
Tons, register	cubic feet	100.0
Tons, shipping	bushels	32.143
	cubic feet	40.0
Tons, short	kilograms	907.18
	pounds, avoirdupois	2,000.0
Watt-hours	Btu	3.413
Watts	Btu per hour	3.415
	horsepower	0.00134
Yards (yd)	chains	0.04545
	fathoms	0.50000
	feet	3.0
	furlongs	0.004545
	inches	36.0
	links	0.22000
	metres	0.9144
	miles, statute	0.000569
	rods	0.18182

Index